PURITAN
PROMENADE

PURITAN

PROMENADE

by Martha Bacon

ILLUSTRATED WITH
PHOTOGRAPHS

1964

HOUGHTON MIFFLIN COMPANY BOSTON

The Riverside Press Cambridge

FIRST PRINTING R

for R. B. B.

ACKNOWLEDGMENTS

I AM INDEBTED to *American Heritage* for permission to reprint "Miss Beecher in Hell" and "The Parson and the Bluestocking." I wish to thank the following for kind cooperation and assistance: the staffs of the Widener Library, Harvard University, the Sterling Memorial Library, Yale University, the John Hay Library and the John Carter Brown Library, Brown University, the library of the University of the Witwatersrand and the Gubbins Africana Library (Johannesburg, South Africa), the New York Public Library, the New Haven Colony Historical Society, the Boston Public Library, the library of the University of Rhode Island, the public library of Peace Dale, Rhode Island, the Johannesburg Public Library, and the Council and Director of the South African Institute of International Affairs, Jan Smuts House.

My mother, Martha Stringham Bacon, has generously allowed me access to all family papers in her private collection.

M. B.

CONTENTS

ILLUSTRATIONS

PURITAN

PROMENADE

YOUR VENT'ROUS AFRIC

Mneme begin. Inspire ye sacred nine,
Your vent'rous Afric in her great design.

FROM "ON RECOLLECTION" BY PHILLIS WHEATLEY

O N JANUARY 4, 1774, the following notice was displayed in the corner of the shop window of a Boston bookseller:

THIS DAY PUBLISH'D

Adorn'd with an elegant engraving of the author
(Price 3s 4d: L. M. Bound)

P O E M S

on various subjects, religious and moral
by Phillis Wheatley, a Negro Girl,
Sold by Messr's Cox and Berry
At their store in King Street

N.B. The subscribers are requested to apply
for their copies.

Like most times, 1774 was scarcely a propitious one for the appearance of slim volumes of verse and this advertised special suffered a fate neither better nor worse than it deserved. It was read by a few interested parties, praised, more for the unusual situation of its author than for any actual merit, dismissed in some quarters and quite soon forgotten. The book was composed largely of doggerel but it exhibited considerable technical proficiency, a working knowledge of the popular verse forms of the day and a familiarity with the classics. Its contents included an ode to Maecenas and one on recollection and an adaptation of Ovid's sixth Metamorphosis, inscribed to the artist Richard Wilson, whose painting of Niobe had inspired the poet to address herself to the same subject. She was no stranger to sorrow and the Niobe legend perhaps struck a sensitive spot in her scarred memory.

The scars were deep ones. Phillis Wheatley had reached the nadir of the human condition. She was a slave, a Negro, a woman and a poet. We search for the poet in Phillis Wheatley because the evidence points to the existence of the creature, glittering and alive beneath the rubble of circumstance and convention. She wrote with an ease that was inescapably self-destructive. The iambics glide on as monotonously and generally as harmlessly as waters of a millstream, without error and anything that could be described as poetic inspiration. Laudatory verses addressed to the great and the near-great, elegies, solemn and pedestrian, to dead clergymen, dead infants, ladies and gentlemen, cut off in the flower, lines ridden with every cliché yielded by her century sprawled from Phillis' goose-quill. Her work was valued in her time for all the wrong reasons by many of the wrong people and some of the right ones. The gifts she had were not so much prostituted as put to a sterile concubinage. Simplicity, natural love, natural anger were all made subservient to an affected morality that was the more lethal to her talents because it was perfectly sincere.

So accommodating a poet could not help but attain within her circle a rising reputation. Phillis' skills were quickly recognized and they were much in demand about Boston. From the age of fourteen on she turned out a considerable body of work, most of it produced on request for appropriate occasions. Appropriate occasions were almost always deaths. The poor child elegised and eulogised, obeying the law of supply and demand, not for gain, not from inspiration, but because the performance was required of her. It is dull stuff and Phillis must have found it dull to write, but the habit of compliance was so imperious that she had no choice but to respond. She seems rarely to have yielded to her own choice of a subject. Here and there she spoke to please herself. There are lines to "A Young African Painter" whose work interested her because he was an African and a little nosegay of verses to "Susannah," Phillis' mistress and foster mother, written as a farewell present when Phillis made her trip to England. In this poem Phillis broke from her customary metrical pattern, the heroic couplet, and wrote a slight lyric, celebrating the excitement of the voyage and a child's regret at leaving home. Elsewhere, with Ovid's text to support her, she struggled toward a statement of unresigned sorrow:

> *No reason her* imperious temper quells*
> *But all her father in her tongue rebels.*

In her "Ode to Maecenas" she dwells with satisfaction on the playwright Terence, also an African and a slave.

---

* Niobe, the daughter of Tantalus.

But I less happy [than Terence] cannot raise the song:
The faltering music dies upon my tongue.

.　.　.　.　.　.　.　.　.　.　.　.　.　.　.

The happier Terence all the choir inspired,
His soul replenished and his bosom fired:
But say, ye Muses, why this partial grace
To one alone of Afric's sable race;
From age to age, transmitting thus his name
With the first glory in the realms of fame?

These examples are exceptions. For the most part the reading public wished only to find itself flattered and cajoled in verse that rhymed and scanned. The doubts and yearnings of slave girls were not calculated to foster self-love in white readers, and Phillis did not subject her audience to much of this kind of thing. She soothed and solaced and celebrated, destroying her gift by maiming it to suit her hearers. There is no doubt that she was gifted. T. S. Eliot has pointed out that promise in a young writer shows first not in originality of idea or emotion but in technical competence. The poet is first apparent in the use of his tools. Phillis used her borrowed tools adroitly and with an occasional flashy gesture. She made of her skill a flattering unction to lay to her soul and was undone as a poet.

Fastidious as a raccoon under his dome at "Monticello," Thomas Jefferson in his later years read and gave vent to an epigram: "Religion produced a Phillis Wheatley," he observed, "but it could not produce a poet."

Dr. Samuel Stanhope Smith in his *Essay on the Causes of*

the Variety of Complexion and Figure in the Human Species disagreed fervently. Dr. Smith challenged the third President of the United States to show "a planter or other master who could equal her." Jefferson, a logical man, who declined to deal with questions which he had not raised, begged the issue. Her poems were beneath the dignity of criticism, he said. He produced no planter and turned to the task of running a roof over the passageway between his kitchen and the slave quarters, thus sparing his dependents a wetting in inclement weather.

The poetry had fared better at the hands of Voltaire, who did not trouble to read it but availed himself of Phillis' reputation in order to make a point when writing to Baron Constant de Rebeq: *"Fontenelle avait tort de dire qu'il n'y aurait jamais des poètes chez les Nègres: il y a actuellement une Nègresse qui fait de très bons vers Anglais."*

To Thomas Clarkson, who submitted his Latin oration on "The Slavery and Commerce of the Human Species, Particularly the African" at Cambridge University in 1785 and gained a first prize, Phillis proved invaluable. He quoted from her copiously to prove his contention that the curse laid upon Ham was nothing more than a monstrous legend and that the enslavement of Africans was carried on in the teeth of divine disapproval. After citing a number of passages from Phillis' poems he concluded sardonically that "if the authoress was designed for slavery (as the argument must confess) the greater part of the inhabitants of Great Britain must lose their claim to freedom."

Phillis' slight fame served every turn but her own. Jupiter Hammon, another Negro with a knack for versification, addressed her rapturously as "the Ethiopian poetess . . . who soon became acquainted with the Gospel of Jesus Christ," adding one more nonsensical clang to the expanding volume of inflated verse — it seems unlikely that Phillis was an Ethiopian and the poem is a very bad one. A young poet, Joseph Ladd, who wrote under the arresting pen name of Arouet, flung a panegyric at her feet before getting himself killed in a duel in North Carolina:

> *Here the fair volume shows the far-spread fame*
> *Of wondrous Wheatley, Afric's heir to fame.*
> *Well is it known what glowing genius shines,*
> *What force of numbers in her polished lines:*
> *With magic power the grand descriptions roll*
> *Thick on the mind and agitate the soul.*

Alexander Pope had much to answer for in making the heroic couplet so available.

Little can be done with the poetry that Phillis Wheatley left to posterity save to lay it decently to rest. It is time-serving and inadequate, the legitimate result of the tractarians and egotists who called it forth and fostered it. And yet Phillis was neither a time-server nor a nonentity. She was the second woman poet in America to be published and one of the earliest of either sex. Had she not been a black female slave facing insoluble problems she might have been a much better poet or she might not have been a poet at all, but clearly she would have been something out of the ordinary. She steps diffidently from a tribal society somewhere south of the Sahara into the margins of our history. Her own is nothing but a cloud of conjecture. She glides into eighteenth-century drawing rooms, a graceful little ornament, and speaks her lines with a half-dozen or more of the men and women who created the drama of the age. She was a member of a "connexion." The memory of John Churchill, Duke of Marlborough, hung over Phillis' patroness, Selina Hastings, a relative-in-law to Warren Hastings. Phillis corresponded with George Washington and justified her claims as a poet in the eyes of John Hancock. She might have satisfied our curiosity more efficiently by choosing herself for subject instead of putting her abilities at the service of her masters. For nothing in her verse gives us a daylight view of her. On the subject of her marriage, the births and deaths of her children, of the grinding poverty in which she died, of prosperous, pious Boston and the roar and stench and finery of eighteenth-century London she had nothing to say. Her poetry seems to have been written with a view to concealing the essential aspects of her existence as a grove of thorn trees conceals the sable antelope. We may scarcely hunt her down. Charming, young, gifted and black, she provokes our attention, as when on the slave block in Boston in 1761, a minute shard of black ivory, she caught the eye of her purchaser, Mrs. Susannah Wheatley.

The story cannot begin at the beginning. Phillis Wheatley would never have spoken as rakishly as Topsy about her origins or lack of them, but like Topsy she was unable to say where she was born. She just appeared — on the Feather Wharf in Boston, wearing a filibeg (a piece of carpeting) and she was guessed to be about six years old "from the circumstance of her shedding her front teeth."

"They came from Angola and the Congo: from Dahomey, Lagos, Old Calabar and the Bonny River: from the

Central Niger and Hausaland, from Portuguese Guinea and the Gabon." They were packed like spoons in the holds to die of starvation and filth or to survive somehow and add their strength to the making of new nations. There was no reason for a child of six to live through even a quarter of what Phillis Wheatley must have endured between the two continents, but she managed it somehow. On a June day in 1761 she was listed with a consignment of blacks to be sold separately or in lots to suit the convenience of the buyer and was knocked down for approximately three pounds to her future mistress.

Susannah Wheatley was the wife of John Wheatley, a prosperous tailor in King Street, then a fashionable residential district now known as State Street. Phillis was to find herself admirably situated. She lived within walking distance of the Old South Church, where she was taught to worship after the strictest sect of the Pharisees. From the Wheatleys' doorstep she could see the lion and the unicorn emblazoned on Government House at the head of the street.

Mrs. Wheatley was reaching middle age, a time of life when one looks with an appreciative eye toward peace and quiet, and she had visited the Feather Wharf in order to purchase for herself "a young Negress to be brought up under her own eye in order that she might secure for herself a faithful domestic in her old age."

The article might have been considered a bit young for Mrs. Wheatley's purposes but it was unusually attractive. The tailor's wife thought the child appeared to be delicate but she could not resist "the modest demeanor and interesting features of the little stranger." She bought her, took her home, laundered her and dressed her out and found that she had a human being on her hands. To do her and the whole family credit, the Wheatleys were quick to grasp this fact.

The child showed an almost alarming intelligence. The Wheatley twins, Nathaniel and Mary, who were eighteen years old, were enchanted with her. By the time autumn had arrived she was chattering English, mimicking the actions of the entire household and giving every sign of an inquiring mind and an excellent disposition. When Mary Wheatley saw the little savage seize a piece of chalk and begin to make scrawls in imitation of writing, the older girl decided that what was required was an education and started to teach the new acquisition to read and write. Phillis took to learning with an enthusiasm that put the average New England scholar to shame and the dunce's stool. Under the gentle and conscientious teaching of Mary and her mother the erstwhile heathen was reading by the time she was ten "astronomy, ancient and modern geography and ancient history, the Bible and heathen mythology." Heathen mythology particularly attracted her. Her verses quiver with classical allusions, and she conceived an early attachment to Pope's Iliad.

Such a phenomenon was not to be wasted in menial labor, at least not in the Wheatley household. All thought of training Phillis for a servant was abandoned and she engaged in no tasks that could be construed as beneath the dignity of a lady: "nor was she allowed to associate with the other domestics of the family who were of her color and condition but was kept constantly about the person of her mistress."

"I was a poor little outcast," Phillis wrote to Obour Tanner, a fellow slave girl, after Mrs. Wheatley's death, "and a stranger when she took me in: not only into her own house but I presently became a sharer in her most tender affections. I was treated by her more like a child than a servant: no opportunity was left unimproved of giving me the best of advice, but in terms how tender, how engaging! . . . I ate of her bread and drank of her cup and was to her as a daughter."

Thanks to Phillis, Mrs. Wheatley emerges for a moment from an almost complete obscurity and we gain a glimpse of a quiet Colonial woman who but for her bondswoman would have vanished into her grave, leaving no wrack behind. Mrs. Wheatley assumes the shape of a woman who could not forego a commitment to a certain child and kept to it until her death. Only this fact singles her out. Mrs. Wheatley expressed no opinions on public matters, nor did she give rein to a creative imagination nor sell all her goods to feed the poor. She and her husband were satisfied members of the mercantile class, gentled by education and delicate living. They were politically conservative and if they were opposed to the Stamp Act on the one hand they appear to have regarded armed rebellion on the other as bad for trade. Nathaniel Wheatley pursued business on both sides of the Atlantic throughout hostilities, never having taken up arms against the mother country. The Wheatleys seem to have had no moral objections to slavery. Mrs. Wheatley visited the Feather Wharf to traffic in human flesh as coolly as a farmer buying cattle at a fair. Her affection for the child was completely partial and personal and the remaining black members of the household had it neither better nor worse than the majority of their kind. Prince, the Wheatley coachman, "that saucy varlet," narrowly missed a flogging for having had the impudence to seat "my Phillis" beside himself on the box rather than inside the coach where she belonged when he had been sent to fetch her home from an evening party.

Mrs. Wheatley and her daughter quickly noticed that with all Phillis' marked abilities to absorb information she had a very unpredictable memory. While she could grasp and recall any amount of material out of a book she was scatterbrained and incoherent when it came to setting down her thoughts. Her woolly head teemed with ideas but they filtered through it as soon as they entered it and Mrs. Wheatley, anxious that no instance of genius should escape, equipped the girl's bedroom with a rushlight and writing materials in order that Phillis might take advantage of any inspiration that might seize her in the middle of the night. Ready to please in all things, Phillis courted inspiration and wrote diligently, addressing an ode even to the traitorous Mneme in which there is not a word to suggest that the writer understands what it is to remember anything of any significance. She could never be brought to recall the fragment of life that she left behind her in Africa. She retained one image: her mother "poured water to the sun at his rising," and beyond this she maintained a silence as secret as that of the leopard, mingling with the light and dark of the African bush.

There could be many reasons for this cutoff, and a likely one is that Phillis may have been captured when scarcely more than an infant and perhaps spent the better part of her first six years marching beside the coffles or running about the barracoons. Whatever her reasons, Phillis concerned herself with the past only when it served her as a rhetorical device, as in her address to Lord Dartmouth, Secretary to the colonies in North America:

> *Should you, My Lord, while you peruse my song*
> *Wonder from whence my love of freedom sprung,*
> *Whence flow these wishes for the common good,*
> *By feeling hearts alone best understood,*
> *I, young in life, by seeming cruel fate*
> *Was snatch'd from Afric's seeming happy seat:*
> *What pangs excruciating must molest —*
> *What sorrows labor in my parent's breast?*
> *Steel'd was that soul and by no misery mov'd*
> *That from a father seiz'd a babe belov'd.*
> *Such, such my case. And can I then but pray*
> *Others may never feel tyrannic sway.*

The poem does not help us to any apprehension of Phillis' father. It merely confirms us in the assumption that she had one. Like all the other lay figures who stalk through her poems he has only the remotest connection with reality. What this poem does make clear, as do several others, is that Phillis, at a very early age, understood her situation and was able to relate it to the political scene. At the age of fourteen she could address George III on the subject of the Stamp Act (this seems to have been her first finished poem) and a little later the students of Harvard

College on the benefits of a university education and know what she was talking about and why. She alluded to her state as a slave but she was too well acquainted with the Westminster Catechism to murmur against the condition to which God had called her. She took comfort in the belief that though in bondage she was an heir to Salvation and saw the blackbirder that had brought her to New England as an instrument of God's mercy, incomparable in its efficiency. Anything rather than exist beyond the reach of the Gospel. Phillis received the Christian religion, humbly, literally and gratefully, as it was taught her, and professed her faith before Dr. Sewell and the elders of the Old South Church in 1769.

This quiet conversion might have been the end of Phillis' story. She might have written her verses, caused a small stir in her neighborhood and died unknown save for a clergyman, or, rather, two clergymen.

A generation before Phillis, in an unregenerate state, had made her appearance on the slave block, New England had been swept by a religious revival, emanating from Northampton, Massachusetts, which sparkled down the river valley and spread to the coastal towns like a forest fire. The person ultimately responsible for this spiritual arson loomed over New England, like Polyphemus, bloody-minded and single-eyed. Jonathan Edwards, applying the empiricism of John Locke to his doctrinaire Calvinism, drew the New England spirit into a dilemma from which there was little chance of escape. Damned from his conception, mankind swung like a threaded spider over the blazing gulfs that yawned for his soul after death. Free will was scarcely more than a cheap trick of the Creator to make his children's fiery fate more sure. Works were of no avail. Only Grace could save and Grace was very illiberally dispensed. Congregations quailed. The doubting and the damned despaired or yielded to apathy. Those who were happy enough to number themselves among the elect bore witness to their state by hallucinations, levitations or falling down and foaming at the mouth. Few people were equipped to deal with Edwards' circle of reasoning which comprehended the argument that the damned themselves must rejoice to feed the flames "if it be to the greater glory of God." The thought was difficult to follow and the implications were as horrifying as a nightmare of Hieronymus Bosch. Controversy raged in the universities and hysteria prevailed among the simple-minded. New England teemed with manifestations of Grace, saintly deathbeds and monstrous children who haunted clergymen's studies and declared themselves when questioned (usually) ready for death.

In a civilization with so little chance of gaining anything by good behavior it is not surprising that a large number of people pursued the course of natural depravity, having little to lose thereby. Business prospered. One might as well be rich in this world, since virtue would not necessarily buy even reasonable comfort in the next. The slave trade prospered in religious New England, and while men and women trembled for their own souls they gave little thought in their panic to the thousands of bodies rotting between the decks of the slavers. It fell to the Quakers and the Evangelicals, to Thomas Clarkson and to Wilberforce to take thought for the black man. And with these stand the erratic, dogged and occasionally absurd figures of the Wesleys and George Whitefield.

Whitefield stormed prisons and pesthouses. He made during his arduous lifetime seven trips to America and he built the orphanage at Bethesda, Georgia, to shelter both black and white. Horace Walpole, a questionable witness, swore that he teased Lady Huntingdon out of her watches and jewels to raise money for it — and he preached to the African as one more sinner to be saved. In this respect the slave did not differ from his master, and men and women of every color and condition flocked to hear this doctrine.

It is easy to see why Whitefield's preaching brought relief to the popular mind. The answer lies not in what Whitefield believed. He stood firmly on the doctrines expounded by Edwards and held with him that the elect were few in number and arbitrarily chosen. But his sermons were short on theology and long on dramatic effects and what would now be described as audience identification. He was a born advertiser and Salvation was his commodity. He produced the usual set piece — nobody need fear heresy — but he begged the issue and spoke to the people as one of themselves. Although he could not promise Heaven as a reward for good conduct he allowed a glimmer of light on the dismal prospect by proposing that good works necessarily stem and follow from election. He even concluded his sermon on "The Eternity of Hell's Punishments" on a soothing note: "Let no sincere Christian be in the least terrified by what has been delivered. No, for you is reserved a crown, a kingdom and an exceeding weight of Glory." For those who considered themselves sincere Christians these were honeyed words, and his hearers gorged themselves on them.

Whitefield's reputation offended the fastidious. They went as often as not to hear and mock and remained to weep and pray. He lacked completely the Dantesque dignity and grievous intellectual splendor of Edwards. He was aggressive and bombastic and loudly self-congratulatory on having, like the Saviour, been born in an inn. He was disfigured by an immovable squint that earned him the lampoon of Dr. Squintum in Samuel Foote's comedy *The Minor*, in which he was heavily burlesqued. He was asthmatic and in later life fat. He bore upon him all the marks of an insuperable and sanctimonious bore but he fed the hungry, clothed the naked, visited those in prison and stopped with them at the gallows' foot. And his showmanship was flawless. Edwards never raised his voice, never gestured while his flock went sizzling to Hell; Whitefield gently roared his hearers like any sucking dove, like any nightingale, straight to Heaven.

He knew what his congregations wanted before they knew it themselves. "Well, my boys," he began when preaching a sermon to the seamen of New York. He proceeded from this breezy opening to broach a noisy and elaborate metaphor, describing life as a stormy sea and creating a vivid image of the soul as a vessel foundering in its surge. "Our masts are gone — what next?" he bellowed. "Take to the long boats, sir," shouted the sailors, and Whitefield, seizing the figure from his audience, made his sermon from the material that it gave him.

He called the desperate colliers of Hanham Mount to

repentance, men in such misery that they had become the terror of the countryside. He was much struck by "the white gutters made by their tears which plentifully fell down their black cheeks as they came from the coal pits." The message lay beneath the ranting like an adder among stones. Repentance and good works were within the province of any man and could in themselves be construed as signals of Grace.

On seven separate visits to America, in the teeth of a steadily gathering and alarmed opposition, Whitefield called the flock and mouthed and bellowed — no velvet mouth but in pure market language — and with unshakable success. In vain were the pulpits of Yale and Harvard closed to him. He preached out of doors. A short-lived friendship with Jonathan Edwards ended in disagreement over the efficacy of "impulses." The foundations of orthodoxy, never very secure in volatile New England, shifted uneasily. The Reverend Thomas Clap swore that Mr. Edwards had told him that the Reverend Mr. Whitefield had said "that it was his design to turn the generality of ministers in the Country out of their places." The New England clergy, its wig sadly awry, could do little but protest, and Whitefield came on and on. He stocked his orphanage with grateful orphans, he continued his attendance at hangings and braved the smallpox epidemic in Boston in 1763–1764. On his seventh visit to America in 1770 he fell ill in Newburyport of a fatal attack of asthma. "I shall die silent," he gasped and made an end. Thousands mourned him as a father, and among them was Phillis Wheatley.

Her facile pen was at the service of his obsequies imme-

diately. She wrote a funeral ode that appeared later with
the sermon which had been delivered at his rites. Here
Whitefield is paraphrased and his patroness in England
praised.

> *Take Him, ye Africans, He longs for you.*
> *Impartial Saviour is his title due:*
> *Washed in the fountain of redeeming blood*
> *Ye shall be sons and kings and priests of God.*
>
> *Great Countess, we Americans revere*
> *Thy name and mingle in thy grief sincere.*
> *New England deeply feels, the orphans mourn,*
> *Their more than father will no more return.*

The great countess was Selina Hastings, Countess of
Huntingdon, and Whitefield had been her chaplain. She
was nicknamed the Queen of the Methodists and her range
of influence among Evangelical preachers was known as
Lady Huntingdon's "connexion." She was a friend to
William Legge, second Earl of Dartmouth, who combined
being president of the board of trade with the acquisition
of Methodism in his early youth. He opened his house in
Cheltenham to Wesley when the pulpits of the Establishment were closed to him. His religion was of an unembar-
rassed order and won him the title of the "Psalm-singer"
when he became Secretary to His Majesty's colonies in
North America. He had advised stern measures with the
colonists during his tenure of office among them and
Phillis Wheatley's address to him pleaded their cause in
terms that were both courteous and flattering. With the
publication of the lines on the death of George Whitefield,

PHILLIS WHEATLEY, NEGRO SERVANT to Mr JOHN WHEATLEY, of BOSTON.

PHILLIS WHEATLEY

"See, look at my Phillis! Does she not seem as though she would speak to me?" (page 23)

Phillis fell under the favorable notice of the "Methodist Court." Her condition as a slave and a Negro added to her attractions. Lady Huntingdon had been much impressed by the moving sermons of the Indian, Samson Occum, whose effusions earned him the sum of forty-five thousand dollars during his tour of England, and whose heart-rending discourse to a fellow Indian about to be hanged was published to vast applause in 1772. Noble savages along with edifying deathbeds were in fashion and Phillis had all the qualifications for noble savagery along with good table manners and a flair for making verses. She was beginning to cut a most desirable figure. She held unexceptionable views and was mindful of her station. She had expressed a polite liberalism in her strictures on the Stamp Act but she advocated no real reversal in the proper order of society. She was perfectly inured to drawing rooms and graced them with style and competence. People more powerful than the Wheatleys and their neighbors were becoming conscious of her.

"Her modesty admirably contrasted with her merit and powerfully increased her charms," says one of her biographers. "She combined excellent kindness of feeling, talent and propriety." She could not fail to win adherents wherever she made an appearance.

The sixteen-year-old girl who was attracting so much interest was no fool. Her work and her manner of conducting her life show that she knew herself to be confronting a brittle, sophisticated and untrustworthy society and she looked for hedges against disaster: to please God and those who for lack of a more precise term must be called her friends, and through the most circumspect behavior to avoid occasions of evil. Like the playwright, Terence, to whom she made her wistful reference, she made it her task not to offend the many while pleasing the *boni*.

She grew up as tenderly nurtured as a young princess, as innocently devout and as eager for the golden tent of God as Blake's little black boy. And like a cloud or a shady grove the sign of Africa was upon her. She was provided with no shield against the future and she had no status save that dealt at random by a whimsical world delighted to play with her as a cat plays with a mouse, tossing it about amorously until it is dead. She could have no durable stake in her environment and there was nothing in her character to help her to harden and grapple with the realities of her situation when it became desperate. She was gentle, affectionate, patient and above all dutiful, "so devoted to her [Susannah Wheatley's] interests as to have no will in opposition to her benefactress."

Because of her superior gifts she was expected to shift her way through a lifetime by gratifying the vanity of those more fortunately placed than herself and on this slender cable hung her only hopes of survival. The avenues of labor were closed to her through lack of training and as a slave she could not have engaged in them to her own profit in any case. The Abbé Grégoire hints that she had her share of intellectual arrogance, encouraged by the flattery of her circle, which further unfitted her for any practical activity, and if this was true it is hardly surprising. She had plenty of cause for more vanity than she ever exhibited.

But the strains under which she labored told early in attacks of asthma and these gave rise to conscientious concern among the Wheatleys. The adopted daughter was solicitously shielded from the night air and received visitors, "among whom were many clergymen" in well-heated drawing rooms. Her admirers gave her books and got poems in return, but in spite of these advantages Phillis was often indisposed for weeks at a time, pining through the New England winters and longing for spring.

She learned early to deal with the problem of patronage. Dr. Johnson's lines to Lord Chesterfield are scarcely more decisive than Phillis' handling of social dilemmas. "Whenever she was invited to the houses of individuals of wealth and distinction," says Margaretta Matilda Odell "(which frequently happened) she always declined the seat offered her at their board, and requesting that a side table be laid for her dined modestly apart from the rest of the company."

"A woman of so much mind as Phillis possessed," continues Miss Odell, "could not but be aware of the emptiness of so many of the artificial distinctions of life. She could not indeed have felt so utterly unworthy to sit down among the guests with those by whom she had been bidden to the banquet . . . by taking the lowest seat at the feast she placed herself where she could certainly expect neither to give nor receive offense."

How otherwise than by an accident of color Phillis could have given offense is a puzzler. Indeed, she might well have requited Virginia Woolf's satirical search for yet one more "lady" in literature to write about along with Miss Edgeworth, Miss Mitford and Miss Austen. She possessed to a marked degree "that indefinable something that marks the lady" that the Misses Brontë in spite of their genius so deplorably lacked. The indefinable something can be a threat to art and is in some cases fatal to it and for better or worse Phillis Wheatley had it.

She was modest, graceful, witty and pretty. She could comply with a funeral ode and she could turn out a rebus. Her contribution to the parlor pleasures of the time throws a little sunlight across the figure of the slave girl. Here is Phillis showing her skill at an eighteenth-century word game:

Phillis' answer to J. B.'s rebus.

The poet asks and Phillis can't refuse
To show the obedience of the Infant Muse.
She knows the Quail of most inviting taste
Fed Israel's army in the dreary waste;
And what on Britain's royal standard's born
But the tall, graceful, rampant Unicorn?
The Emerald with a vivid verdure glows
Among the gems which regal crowns compose;
Boston's a town, polite and debonair
To which the beaux and beauteous nymphs repair.
Each Helen strikes the mind with sweet surprise
While living lightening flashes from her eyes.
See young Euphorbus of the Danaan line
By Menelaus' hand to death resign:
The well known peer of popular applause
Is C —— m, zealous to support our laws.

And the whole is:

Quebec, *now vanquished must obey,*
She too must annual tribute pay
To Britain of immortal fame,
And add new glory to her fame.

There is a portrait of Phillis, the same engraving that adorned her poems, which suggests that her appearance was charming. She sits upright at her writing desk, a spritely little figure, with large, bright eyes, a tilted nose and a small baroquely curved mouth. Her back is straight as whalebone can make it and an air of tension pervades the little figure, implying a high degree of vitality. The picture is in a conventional mode of the time — a slightly idealized (possibly) portrait of a young bluestocking, pen, paper, and all. Phillis' erect head is crowned with a white-ruffled cap. Mrs. Wheatley considered the likeness excellent. "See, look at my Phillis! Does she not seem as though she would speak to me?" she exclaimed when the portrait was put in her hands during Phillis' absence in England.

Charming, talented and elegantly mannered as she undoubtedly was, Phillis showed a good deal of sense in her choice of a separate table. Any study of the manners and morals of the gentlemen of the time and many of the ladies — Phillis mingled only with gentlemen and ladies — would suggest that a virgin of questionable ancestry, uncertain means and dependent on the private virtues of mortal protectors, no matter what her color, was doing little better than Jonathan Edwards' spider hanging by a thread over the chasm. It is reasonable to suppose that Phillis had read *Pamela* and it would have been natural for her to identify herself with that distracted heroine. Innocent, attractive, chaste and a slave, she was a natural subject for insult and attempted seduction and her complexion gave her no more than a criminal's franchise in the world. She had no armor against the importunities of any drunken young buck from a rich merchant's family — it would have been much to ask that John Wheatley or his son, Nathaniel, should defend her honor should it be impugned. Fastidious, refined and impeccably pious, Phillis took no risks. And beyond the logical caution which her decision to separate herself from her fellow guests implies, the aristocrat lodges like a panther in the brush. Only a fool seeks out conflicts with impudence, and a lady and an aristocrat is only rude on purpose. There is a challenging element of ladylike rudeness in Phillis' refusal to accept the company of her masters who had singled her out from her fellow prisoners. There is no record of her having disclaimed the companionship of white people in England, where since the year 1705 no human being could be called a slave.

Phillis Wheatley paid her visit to England in 1773 under fairly impressive auspices. As a minor celebrity she traveled under the protection of her foster brother, Nathaniel, who was journeying to London in the interests of the family business. Lord Dartmouth, the "Psalm-singer," who in two years' time would be appointed Lord Privy Seal, was prepared to receive the poet, and Lady Huntingdon could scarcely resist so interesting a subject.

Phillis' sea voyage in 1773 took approximately three months to complete. It was the culmination of a longer one that carried her from the stone-age life of an African village to the era and the city which brought forth *The Castle of Otranto* and the *Letters* of Lord Chesterfield (who shared Phillis' admiration for George Whitefield, although on somewhat different grounds), *Rasselas* and *The Rake's Progress*, John Wilkes' seditious libel, *The Songs of Innocence* and *The Marriage of Heaven and Hell*.

She saw the paintings of Richard Wilson, she met aristocrats at a garden party given in her honor and shared the Countess of Huntingdon's pew in chapel. She responded precisely as an eighteenth-century heroine with Methodist leanings might have been expected to do, cutting an elegant figure in the process. "The vast variety of scenes that have passed before us . . . will serve to convince us of the uncertain duration of all things temporal, and the proper result of such a consideration is an ardent desire of a preparation for a state and enjoyments which are more suitable to the immortal mind."

So much for the temptations of world.

The Countess of Huntingdon, the daughter of Washington Shirley of Stanton in Leicestershire, was at the time of Phillis' visit nearly seventy years old. She was rich, had married well and was herself well born. Her Methodism had attacked her early in life and had somewhat excluded her from the centers of high life, although her relatives and her husband's friendship with Bolingbroke and Chesterfield held her within the framework of that society. She had from an early age given herself to the education of the poor and she had a desire "to reform the morals of persons of her own class." To do her justice, there was need for improvement, but Selina had little success in most quarters. One of her most notorious failures was with her cousin, the mad Lord Ferrers ("mad perhaps but not mad enough to listen to my lady's sermons," said Horace Walpole). Phillis Wheatley moved among people who had paled at the news of Lord Ferrers' dissipations and remembered his trip to the gallows for the murder of his servant.

Condemned by a jury of his peers, some of them wearing the now ragged robes which had served their forebears at the trial of the Queen of Scots, Lord Ferrers was carried to Tyburn in a black landau, drawn by six black horses, and died a richly deserved death at the end of a silken rope.

His cousin, the Queen of the Methodists, was a hard-featured do-gooder whose vagaries leave little room for wonder that some of her relatives ran mad. She spent huge sums of money endowing Methodist colleges and politicked to have her daughter, Lady Elizabeth Hastings, named a lady of the bedchamber, only to undo the good work because she would not countenance the girl's playing cards on Sundays. She withdrew her cousin's playing cards, reduced his measure of wine after his condemnation and was rigid in her opposition to the visits paid him in prison by his mistress. Her manner of dressing was the wonder and admiration of all. Mrs. Pendarvis, a celebrated gossip at the court of George II, was continuously struck by Lady Huntingdon's gowns and thought them worth recording: "a most labored piece of finery, the pattern much properer for a stucco staircase than the apparel of a lady . . . a gown embroidered with all the beasts of the Book of Revelations from lion to serpent."

Lady Huntingdon is one of those maddening figures who will not content herself with being merely ridiculous. "In truth," wrote the aged Sarah, Duchess of Marlborough, to Selina, at the time a comparatively young woman, "I always feel more happy and contented with you than after a whole week's round of amusements." To a complaint that Lady Huntingdon usurped the office of a bishop,

George II only replied that he wished he had more bishops like her.

Her kindness to Phillis was genuine. She treated the little African with generosity and respect, and it was through her influence that the volume of poems was first published by Aldgate in London in 1773 with an appropriate dedication.

Phillis' tribute had been palpably welcome. The Countess was not averse to seeing herself in heroic guise and a volume of verse on her altars was consonant with grandeur and could stand worthily beside what Horace Walpole referred to as the "beatific print." In this engraving Selina Hastings is depicted in semi-Greek attire, her hard features somewhat softened to conform with the ideals of the age, resolutely trampling a coronet.

Stucco staircase or egalitarian angel, the countess served Phillis Wheatley well and her young friend was grateful. Phillis met with unfailing condescension. A retired Lord Mayor of London, Brook Watson, presented her with a copy of *Paradise Lost*, the only one of all her books that she kept by her until her death, and she narrowly missed an encounter with George III.

Phillis, as her verses show, was quite prepared to be a loyal subject to the King, provided he modified his demands on the colonies, and would no doubt have performed as creditably for Queen Charlotte as she did for Lady Huntingdon. But the sojourn in England was cut short by bad news. Mrs. Wheatley was ailing. Phillis and Nathaniel, on hearing these tidings, took ship as soon as possible, arriving in America only in time to receive Mrs. Wheatley's last words and blessings.

The blow fell heavily on Phillis. With Susannah Wheatley's death she lost her chief protector. Mary Wheatley had married the reverend John Lothrop in 1771 and had assumed new responsibilities as the wife of the young pastor of the Old South Church. Nathaniel and his father were committed to their trade and the anxieties of the worsening political situation. Phillis continued to live under their charge but no provision was made for her future and she moved henceforward in danger.

The poems, thanks to the Countess of Huntingdon, had made their appearance and caused their little stir. The stir inevitably resolved itself into the question as to whether Phillis was or was not a fraud perpetrated on the public by the Wheatleys for their own ends. It was argued that no Negro could have produced such accomplished verse. Designed expressly for the hewing of wood and the drawing of water it was in defiance of all logic and all theology that one of these mechanisms should take to imitating Alexander Pope. The case was argued in and about Boston with tempers rising on all sides. In their own interest the Wheatleys were forced to ask for a trial. Miss Phillis was required to submit to an examination to determine her qualifications for having written her book. A group of eighteen gentlemen of Boston waited on Phillis and her master in the house in King Street and there plied the girl minutely with questions on Scripture, Latin and classical mythology. With her usual docility she answered them, triumphing over their skepticism and winning their unqualified approval. The eighteen gentlemen were astonished — and convinced. One of them was John Hancock. With all the solemnity that the occasion required, they affixed their signatures to a document which in effect gave Phillis Wheatley leave to write as much poetry as she pleased.

> *We, whose names are underwritten do assure the world that the poems specified in the following pages were (as we verily believe) written by Phillis, a young Negro girl, who but a few years since, was brought an uncultivated barbarian from Africa and has ever since been and now is, under the disadvantage of serving as a Slave in a family in this town. She has been examined by some of the best judges and has been thought qualified to write them.*

The book with this seal of approval was received with all the interest usually accorded to freaks. The Abbé Grégoire states in his essay *De la Littérature des Nègres* that they were valued "*d'une manière distinguée*" and disarms criticism (Jefferson's) by citing the author's "*moeurs aimables*," her "*sensibilité exquise*," and "*talents précoces*." Indulgence to a slave girl of nineteen, he points out, is no more than justice.

George Washington, it appears, was of the same opinion. The young lady favored him with an ode on October 26, 1775, and though he was pressed for time he wrote a little belatedly to thank her for it on February 28, 1776, from Craigie House in Cambridge, then his headquarters.

> *Mrs. Phillis:*
> *Your favor of the 26th of October did not reach my hands till the middle of December. Time enough, you will say to have given an answer ere this.*

Granted. But a variety of important occurrences continually interposing to distract the mind and withdraw the attention I hope will apologise for the delay and plead my excuse for the seeming but not real neglect. I thank you for your polite notice of me in the elegant lines you enclosed; and however undeserving I may be of such encomium and panegyric, the style and manner exhibit a striking proof of your poetical talents; in honor of which, and as a tribute justly due you I would have published the poem, had I not been apprehensive that while I only want to give the world this new instance of your genius, I might have incurred the imputation of vanity. This and nothing else determind me not to give it a place in the public prints. If you should ever come to Cambridge or near Headquarters, I shall be happy to see a person so favored by the muses and to whom Nature has been so liberal and so beneficent in her dispensations.

I am with great respect your obt' and humble servant,

GEORGE WASHINGTON.

The ode was certainly all that anyone might have wished as an encomium, and it made a bold attempt at high rhetoric.

> *Thee first in peace and honor we demand*
> *The Grace and Glory of thy martial band.*
> *Famed for thy valor, for thy virtues more,*
> *Hear every tongue thy guardian aid implore.*

It is quite grand — almost Roman. When Henry Lee presented the resolutions to the House of Representatives on the death of General Washington in 1799 it vanished neatly into "First in war, first in peace, and first in the

hearts of his countrymen." But Lee's audience allowed
Phillis a share in the speech and it was generally acknowledged that the seed of the epigram lodged with her like a
pit in a peach, to flower elsewhere and at another time.

But the muses, as Phillis might have put it, did not
prosper in America at the time of the Rebellion nor did
her fortunes. According to the Abbé Grégoire, Phillis
was manumitted in 1775, although the evidence for this
event hangs on the fact that she was not sold up with the
household goods when John Wheatley's business declined.
She continued in the care of the Wheatley family, loved
and valued by Mary Lothrop, writing poetry and hoping
to find applicants for more copies of her book. Religion
occupied her mind and sustained her spirit and she found
solace in the friendship of Obour Tanner.

Obour was a slave girl about ten years older than Phillis
and, like the younger woman, had received an education
from her owners. When she was a very old woman she
told Harriet Beecher Stowe that she thought that she and
Phillis had made the journey to America in the same slave
ship. Obour also believed that she recognized Phillis when
the two met in Newport during the summer of 1770 when
Mary Wheatley spent a season in the watering place and
brought Phillis with her as maid-companion. Whether or
not the acquaintance began with the Middle Passage, as the
slave route was called, is not definitely known, but it is clear
that Phillis and Obour derived great satisfaction from the
interchange. If they had not traveled on the same ship they
nevertheless shared a common fate and had grounds for
communication. Characteristically, Phillis' letters make no

reference to the past. They are principally concerned with religion. She indulged in long paragraphs, turning her sentences as the fashion dictated, purling away like a pious little teakettle. From time to time she boiled up into bubbles of theology but the horror of New England Calvinism was not upon her. The comforts of the "connexion" and the realities of her life as an exile and a slave may have combined to save her from the common obsession of most New Englanders. Or possibly some unconquerable optimism, some sweetness of disposition led her to dwell on the Everlasting Mercy rather than the horrendous possibilities of the wrath to come. Any African slave had worse things to fear than God or Satan. She made her acts of propitiation to men rather than their Creator. In her joyful acceptance of the benefits of the Gospel she resembles another African, Ignatius Sancho, born on a slave ship in 1729. Sancho was purchased on a whim by an Englishman in Cartagena and given as a present to the buyer's three maiden aunts, who lived in Greenwich. His quick wits and engaging ways brought him freedom and comfort. He became a friend to David Garrick and to Laurence Sterne, and ended his eventful life a prosperous man with a numerous family and a soul at peace. He had no use for dissenters, being a devoted Anglican, and he regarded "enthusiasm" of any kind with suspicion; but of the Christian faith he had but one thing to say: "I am clear [that] every good affection, every sweet sensibility, every heartfelt joy, humanity, politeness, charity, all — all are streams from that sacred spring."

Phillis would have concurred, and one must suppose that Obour shared such views. When Phillis fell on evil days

Obour's side of the correspondence vanished, but there is nothing in Phillis' letters to suggest that the two girls were not in complete harmony. The exchange is glib, stylized, elaborate and without conflict. It grapples with religious questions, but the dark night of the soul, agony and redemption, the spiritual life, are reduced to a set of splendid simplicities ornamented with verbal flourishes. A generation later the daughter of Jeremiah Day of Yale would quake at the concept of the worm that dieth not, addressing her religious poems to the implacable image of the New England idolatry and conscious in her sheltered existence of nothing so real as eternal punishment. While Phillis lived the poet Cowper, tormented by the exhortations of the repentant slave captain, John Newton, wallowed in the ecstasies of damnation. Olaudah Equiano, like Phillis an African, writhed in the process of his conversion and lamented that he could not contrive to keep more than eight out of ten of the Commandments. But Phillis Wheatley kept the whole ten with perfect ease and shared with Obour Tanner, who carried the scars of the driver's whip to her grave, the belief that they themselves were clearly of the elect. Phillis had an ontological proof. Would God have brought them out of Africa, the land of the heathen, had he intended anything else? The tone of her letters is on the whole more congratulatory than otherwise.

Dear Sister — [*she wrote Obour in 1778*]
I received your favor of February 6th for which I give you my sincere thanks. I greatly rejoice with you in that realizing view, and I hope experience of

the saving change which you so emphatically describe. Happy were it for us if we could arrive at that Evangelical repentance and the true holiness of heart which you mention. Inexpressibly happy could we be could we have a due sense of the beauties and excellence of the crucified Savior. In His Crucifixion may be seen the marvelous displays of Grace and Love, sufficient to invite us to the rich and endless treasures of His Mercy; let us rejoice in and adore the wonders of God's infinite love in bringing us from a land semblant of darkness itself, where the divine light of revelation (being obscur'd) is as darkness. Here the knowledge of the true God and eternal life are made manifest; but there profound ignorance overshadows the land. Your observation is true, namely that there was nothing in us to recommend us to God [Obour seems to have "observed" a straightforward piece of Calvinist theology]. Many of our fellow creatures are pass'd by when the bowels of divine compassion expanded toward us. May this goodness and long-suffering of God lead us to unfeign'd repentance.

And so forth. God's mercy in bringing us to a land of enlightenment to our ultimate salvation makes it clear that we are objects of his special favor. This is the theme that both girls explored and rationalized to their satisfaction. They were part of the great design and therein lay a contentment that no earthly sorrow, no humiliating ordeal could destroy. In this pleasant tone of voice the correspondence rippled on uninterrupted for some months. There is a lament over the loss of Mrs. Wheatley, and Phillis refers several times to her own uncertain health.

There is nothing private about the collection. The letters seem to have been written in the light of a determination to offend nobody and with a view to making them suitable to almost any eyes. Little that is personal or immediate to Phillis intrudes upon her lofty reflections. If her surroundings and her friends either entertained or oppressed her she did not mention it. For all the picture that these documents give of her world and her times she might have been writing them from the middle of the moon to a point in outer space. She strikes a different note only at the conclusion of the correspondence. A new character is introduced. Obour's meditations were sometimes delivered by hand and Phillis made use of the same messenger when returning answers to her friend. "The young man by whom this is handed to you seems to me to be a very clever young man, knows you well and is very complaisant and agreeable."

The young man was a free Negro named John Peters. He had read a little law and had defended Negroes before the Massachusetts Bar, but he was no defender of himself. In the eyes of most of his contemporaries and of Phillis' friends he invaded her scene briefly as a scandal and a failure. Obour Tanner had nothing to say of him save that Phillis "lowered" herself by marrying him. She quavered her regret to Mrs. Stowe that she had been the instrument that brought the couple together.

He was talented, haughty and handsome. He had picked up the tag ends of an education — along with the law a little medicine, the rudiments of seamanship and somewhere the address of a gentleman. He was a dandy who wore a wig and carried a cane, and for these misdemeanors he was much criticized although John Hancock did the same. When he pleaded the cases of defendants of his own color Josiah Quincy declared himself much impressed by the young African's eloquence and style. He may well have appeared to Phillis not only as a suitable candidate for her husband but as a unique one. He had a reputation for ruthlessness in his law practice, but in view of the condition of most of his clients he could hardly have wrung much money from them. Phillis' friends had doubts of his character and advised her against him. But Phillis was running out of friends in 1778. Mary Lothrop had died with her second baby and her husband did not live much longer. Nathaniel Wheatley, harassed by business matters in the midst of the war, was in London. Phillis married Peters in August 1778 and never drew another breath in peace.

The new nation had been at war for three years. The hardships of the third winter of the Rebellion in Boston were so intolerable that there was a wholesale exodus to the south of people whose chief preoccupation was to find food. Phillis was not in the situation of the healthy Negro woman whose manner of earning a living during this disastrous period was recorded by B. B. Thatcher in his biographical notice of Phillis. This sturdy individual, a free woman, gave birth to and sold babies as fast as she could produce them, asking up to eight dollars for her eldest child, a healthy girl of thirteen suitable for domestic labor. The Peters family, like others in their position, moved to Wilmington in the hope of discovering better conditions. During this painful period Phillis bore two children, both of whom died. Her pitiful attempts to make money by her pen were worse than useless.

"People had other things to attend to than prose or poetry," remarked a niece of Mrs. Wheatley's with whom Phillis lodged briefly on her return from Wilmington. She tried to earn money by opening a small school and Peters got himself a grocery store. Nothing worked. The war was over but the world had changed. Old friends were dead or dispersed. In one or two cases Phillis hesitated to approach for help acquaintances who had frowned on her ill-judged marriage in happier days. Her husband's promising youth came to nothing, she was too proud to beg and unequal to work, and a swift society simply engulfed the Peters family and swept it to confusion. Peters was accused of being above manual labor and of selling his wife's books and papers to find food and fuel during the desolate winters that followed the war. The Abbé Grégoire declares that he abused her in his exasperation at her inefficiency and bluestocking airs and contempt for household tasks. With this *enfant gâtée* on his hands he took to idleness and drink. Phillis' asthma became acute and she fell ill of consumption. A third child was born and some charitable persons, aware of the straits she was in, visited her only to find the exquisite Phillis Wheatley "reduced to a condition too loathsome to describe" and obviously dying. She had scarcely a possession left save her copy of *Paradise Lost*, given her in her days of triumph by Brook Watson.

In 1784 a passerby observed a funeral procession making its way to the Old South Church and upon inquiring he learned that the cortege, which was of the humblest kind, was for "an adult and a child." One of the mourners told him that the dead were Phillis Wheatley and her last baby, who had died with her and was buried in her arms in the churchyard in an unmarked grave.

Peters survived her by three years, a wretched man who styled himself a gentleman and who "proved utterly unworthy of the distinguished woman who honored him with her alliance." His unworthiness seems incontestable. His character cannot be saved but the circumstances must be allowed to be extenuating. A Negro boy of spirit, flung free and half educated on the eighteenth-century world, must have faced difficulties that would have broken better men than Peters. The charge that he abused Phillis is based upon the evidence that he drank and that the Peters family dissolved in misery because of his failure to provide. The sternest eyewitness against Peters is Obour Tanner and his one halfhearted advocate is Josiah Quincy. To walk like a gentleman, to wear a wig and carry a cane, to be talented and a wastrel, to die in jail of debt and fever: these things make of Peters an eighteenth-century stock character, a member of the play, but scarcely a villain. He is simply the logical result of circumstances over which he had little or no control, as was Phillis.

Fate dealt harshly with Phillis Wheatley and posterity cannot help her poetry. Jefferson has the last word on this point. She does not bear comparison with any authentic poet, although to rank her achievement below that of Lydia Huntley Sigourney as did Lydia Child seems unjust. Her native quickness was certainly equal to Mrs. Sigourney's and she had dignity and restraint which the

other totally lacked. "Phyllis' poems do credit to nature —
and put art — merely as art — to the blush," wrote Ignatius
Sancho in 1778. "It [Phyllis' book] reflects nothing to the
glory or generosity of her master — if she is still his slave
— except he glories in the *low vanity* of having in his
wanton power a mind animated by Heaven — a genius
superior to himself. The list of splendid, titled, learned
names in confirmation of her being the real authoress —
alas! shows how very poor the acquisition of wealth and
knowledge is — without generosity, feeling and humanity.
These good, great folks all know — and perhaps admired
— nay praised genius in bondage and then like the priests
and the Levites in sacred writ passed by — not one good
Samaritan among them."

All this is true and irrelevant and Sancho should have
known this because he knew good writing when he saw it,
but in the case of Phillis Wheatley ardor and generosity
carried him away. Sitting in his London grocery store in
Charles Street and scribbling his letters to his numerous
correspondents he seldom failed to fall prey to ardor and
generosity. It is a temptation to draw a parallel between
Phillis and Sancho since they were both Africans and had
been slaves and they both had found their way into the
suburbs of English literature. The similarity ends there.
Phillis had no more and no less in common with Ignatius
Sancho than she had with any other minor figure of her
generation. They both, with hundreds of others, shared a
manner and a number of attitudes inseparable from the
times they lived in. Sancho wrote to a wide number of
friends on an even wider range of subjects: the American

war, a troublesome affair, although he shared with Horace
Walpole the view that America carried within her the
seeds of a classic greatness. He wrote on love, on painting,
the theater, and on Swift, Sterne (his idol) and on Fielding.
He wrote on cruelty to animals, which enraged him; he
would have had people who abused their donkeys impressed
in the King's service. He advised the government on a
means of reducing the national debt: let the aristocracy
donate its plate to the Treasury, keeping back the knives
and forks but parting with the useless and ostentatious
articles that decked their sideboards. He pleaded in the
pages of the *Advertiser* for the life of the unfortunate
Dr. Dodd, the cleric who was hanged for the passing of
forged notes. From the window of his shop he watched
and described while watching the No Popery Riots of
1780, "the worse than Negro barbarity of the populace"
on its way to the burning of Lord Mansfield's library and
the storming of Newgate. He had what Phillis lacked, an
eye for the world he lived in and a writer's compulsion to
tell someone about it. Our legacy of eighteenth-century
letters is the richer for his little sheaf. His enjoyment
of a rhetorical flourish even lends enchantment to his
rodomontade.

Phillis might more reasonably be compared to Olaudah
Equiano, who published his fascinating *Narrative* in 1792.
He wrote diligently, he even attempted verse, he was an
ardent Christian of the Methodist persuasion. But the
fascination lies in the facts of Equiano's story. He must
have been one of the first Africans to describe Greenland,
a country he took for the North Pole, but the hand of the

editor flattens Equiano into incredibility. He scarcely emerges at all save in the breakage of two out of Ten Commandments. Further, both Sancho and Equiano were not only Africans but free Englishmen and taxpayers and Equiano held a post under the government as agent for the Poor Blacks; Phillis was not only a slave but a New England woman.

We dare not look at her in the harsh light of other stronger poets but we may see her outline more clearly if we set her beside another New England woman, more obscure than she and sharing with her the impulse to poetry.

The president of Yale, Jeremiah Day, son-in-law to Roger Sherman, had a daughter, Martha. She was of a later generation than Phillis and imitated Byron and Coleridge rather than Pope. But, like Phillis, she sacrificed her talent to a pious acquiescence in an intolerable state of life. Martha Day was as crushed under the weight of Calvinism as Phillis Wheatley was shaped to the necessities of slavery. Of the two Martha Day was the more sophisticated but she yearned with Phillis for the fanciful and the mythological. She worked long and lovingly over a fable of Noah's dove, which, being changed into a sea-sprite, falls in love with a mortal girl whom he steals from her home and keeps forever in a cave in the sea.

Such frivolities were no more suitable to the pen of a serious Christian than were the possible poems that Phillis Wheatley abjured in favor of her adulatory verse, ground out for a public whose pleasure was her only hold on a place in society. But if Phillis was bound to please the *boni,*

Martha Day confronted an even more formidable audience, in whose eyes such trifling activities were almost certainly displeasing and on whose good will depended the soul's dubious footing in Eternity. Every human activity must turn toward God and His word, but the case was a hard one. "I feel that I ought to be more interested in religion," wrote Martha Day, "but the Bible is to me all darkness." Nevertheless she wrote for God, setting aside her fairy tales.

> *The steadfast earth, the strong untiring sea,*
> *Their verdant isles, their mountains high and hoary,*
> *With awe and fear, shall from thy presence flee,*
> *Then shalt thou sit a judge, the guilty dooming*
> *To adamantine chains and endless fire.*
> *Oh Father, how may we abide thy coming?*
> *Where find a shelter from Jehovah's ire?*

Martha Day put poetry aside lest she offend God. Phillis wrote bad poetry to please men. Too slight for the music that they knew of but could not render, their voices sound wanly in our ears as the spring peepers, wistful, monotonous but an indisputable sound of the landscape of America.

THE WEEPING WILLOW

AND THE ANTIMACASSAR

POLITICS MAKE strange bedfellows. So do religions. The progeny are stranger yet. In the year 1782 when the *Royal George* sank with twice four hundred men aboard her she also sent to the bottom four hundred women of the town and an equal number of Bibles. The women of the town were a common occurrence on warships in the eighteenth century. The Bibles, at least in such numbers, were something new. They had been distributed on the day before the disaster by the Military and Naval Bible Society, one of many branches of the Evangelical movement. This movement had sprung from Methodism and was sprawling uncontrollably over all of England and the United States. Evangelicalism was responsible for both great things and small, for the agitation for the abolition of slavery, for the Society for the Prevention of Cruelty to Animals, for cancer hospitals, for orphanages, for temperance societies, for Sunday School hymns and anti-tobacco leagues. To the "true religion" such families as the Cadburys and the Huntleys and Palmers, Evangelicals to a man,

owe their prosperity. Smoke and spirits gave way to chocolate biscuits while souls were saved, presumably as the con-
sumer munched and the producer grew rich. Evangelicalism
also launched the best-seller on the world.

There had been of course previous best-sellers. In the
year 1662 Michael Wigglesworth brought out a volume of
verse appetizingly entitled *The Day of Doom*. It was
printed in Cambridge, Massachusetts, and was an instanta-
neous success. It was not much more than a rhymed
compilation of New England theology, and its purpose
was to make the nightmare beliefs cherished in the colonies
readily accessible to memory and comprehension. It scared
children into fits and sold steadily and well for about a
century.

One hundred and fourteen years intervened between the
publication of Michael Wigglesworth's entertaining and
instructive work and the rise of the Republic. During that
time Americans had few books. Even had they had many
a large number of people would not have been able to
read them. In England the state of literacy was proportion-
ately worse. But by the end of the first quarter of the
nineteenth century matters had mended. The Age of
Elegance had come to a close. The Age of Reform, with
the Evangelicals in the vanguard, had reached its apogee
and with the Age of Reform the common reader came into
his own. The common reader required writers to improve
his leisure. Certain authors discovered that while he had no
objection to being improved he also wished to be entertained. The formidable Mrs. Hannah More, the friend of
Dr. Johnson and William Wilberforce, sold two million

copies of her *Cheap Repository Tracts* in the year 1795. Their appeal was immediate and all but universal. Mrs. More described them accurately as "cheap literature that would urge piety and subordination in an attractive form, suitable to the people." And the same could be said of all her other works designed to edify the poor. "It is as vulgar as the heart could wish but it is intended only for the most vulgar class or readers," she declared contentedly.

People do not buy and read two million copies of anything merely to improve the character. Mrs. More, in her determination to keep the poor poor but religious, took the most practical way of doing it and gave them stories with plenty of reader-identification. Bad as her stories are, they are in their strange way, "attractive." Mrs. More could tell a story. She couldn't help telling a story. Her morality revolts us, her style is odious but her tale runs along. The reader is involved. *The Shepherd of Salisbury Plain*, not only the most appalling of Mrs. More's sublime works but very possibly the most appalling of all works in the Evangelical strain, nevertheless persuades us to turn its pages. For a moment we believe in that benign clergyman, Mr. Johnson, stopping to talk to the shepherd at twilight. We can see the children plucking the wool from the bushes to bring home for carding. In its queer way the stuff is believable. People read it and asked for more; and they got what they asked for.

Mrs. More not only supplied the populace with moral tales. She and her sister opened schools and taught the poor to read. It was a dangerous thing to do, and Mrs. More realized that in her fight for literacy she was handling a two-edged sword, for people who could read the Bible might also read *The Rights of Man, The Social Contract* and ultimately *Corinne.* Mrs. More conscientiously abstained from teaching her humble scholars to write. Instead she wrote for them and helped to establish from that time forth a large, voracious body of readers who would swallow any amount of sermonizing provided it was encased in fiction. By the year 1820 there were enough popular writers to satisfy the expanding leisure time of two great nations with literate populations. Popular writers emerged from kitchen and hearth, from counting house and manufacturers' office to improve the public mind and to beguile its idle hours. The writers which this public took to its bosom were in many instances women. They wrote fluently and prolifically. They wrote tracts, dramas, stories, essays and poetry. They were industrious and ambitious and with the exception of a few they regarded themselves as poets. In justice it must be said that they did so with reason. An enthusiastic body of readers loved them and all their works and the bays crowning their brows went to them by common acclaim.

In England Maria Edgeworth and Felicia Dorothea Hemans, to name but two, captured the general fancy. America rejoiced in Hannah Flagg Gould, Lydia Maria Child, and above all Lydia Huntley Howard Sigourney, "the American Mrs. Hemans," the "Sweet Singer of Hartford" and the first poetess in the United States.

Why should we single out Mrs. Sigourney for discussion? Why not talk instead of Mrs. Child or Miss Gould? There are plenty of obscure American females who wrote poetry and pleasing moral tales, and many of them wrote better than she did. But not one delighted so vast a public or caused so many luxurious tears to flow or addressed so many public monuments, human and otherwise, to say nothing of private individuals including everyone and everything from missionaries in Burma to geese and even mops and brooms and discarded rags. She comforted people in their bereavements, spurred them to be better than themselves and brought courage and resignation to thousands, while in the rueful phrase of Mr. W. H. Auden, "Poetry [stood] helplessly and impotently by."

"Glossily ringletted and monumentally breast-pinned," as Henry James described her, Mrs. Sigourney was scarcely "serious" in the Evangelical sense. She was born too late to burn with the apostolic zeal of the Clapham sect. She was merely nominally and practically pious. She adhered only tenuously to the notion that suffering is of no import- ance in comparison to the sin which it punishes and carried on with her narrative or her verse, letting the sermon more or less preach itself. Like Mr. Cadbury's chocolate biscuit, her work was palatable, nonintoxicating, sold widely and could be absorbed easily by almost anyone. And there was a great deal of it. Before she died at the age of seventy-four she had inserted herself between the covers of sixty-odd volumes of prose and poetry.

Lydia Sigourney did not write faulty poetry or weak poetry or the kind of poetry that nobody could understand, nor did she, precisely speaking, fail to write poetry. She rhymed and scanned along with Byron, Coleridge and Wordsworth, borrowing their rhythms and their cadences where it suited her, committing her act of violence against the living literature with so much adroitness and conviction that money and fame crowned the successful effort by return of post. What she turned out was atrocious, abysmal, dreadnought poetry that obeyed the rules governing grammar and syntax — if you weren't too particular — and those regulations drawn up for the purposes of reducing human emotions to a solution of sugar and water laced with molasses.

The existence of genuine poetry in America proved no deterrent. For all that it meant to Lydia Sigourney and her readers it might as well not have existed at all. It was nothing to them that Joseph Rodman Drake had written his mock epic *The Culprit Fay* and proved to his doubting friends that the American landscape could yield an authentic poem. He had executed with grace and skill a fantasy, something akin to Michael Drayton's fairy poem *Nymphidia*, but the woods and streams of the Hudson River Valley served him for a scene. It is worth quoting here to show one of the American talents against which Lydia Sigourney measured her strength.

> *He put his acorn helmet on;*
> *It was plumed of the silk of the thistledown;*
> *The corselet plate that guarded his breast*
> *Was once the wild bee's golden vest;*
> *His cloak, of a thousand mingled dyes,*
> *Was formed of the wings of butterflies;*
> *His shield was the shell of a lady-bug queen,*
> *Studs of gold on a ground of green;*
> *And the quivering lance which he brandished bright,*

Was the sting of a wasp he had slain in a fight.
Swift he bestrode his fire-fly steed;
He bared his blade of the bent grass blue;
He drove his spurs of the cockle seed,
And away like a glance of thought he flew,
To skim the heavens and follow far
The fiery trail of a rocket star.

There were not only poets to be reckoned with but criticism too had raised its gorgon's head in the person of Edgar Allan Poe. Poe's lyrical powers were only a portion of his literary accoutrements. He had unleashed his furies against the imprecisions and inadequacies of the younger William Ellery Channing and stood guard over American writing, but for one reason or another he permitted Mrs. Sigourney a place among the poets. Lydia Sigourney pursued her course complacently and with profit for roughly forty-five years, shrilling her sentiments and her shibboleths to her satisfied hearers while the strains of Herman Melville and Emily Dickinson died on the air.

The collapse of her reputation was relatively swift. Indeed the only poetic aspect of her history resides in the rough justice with which she was consigned to oblivion. There is no rehabilitation in store for her. Re-evaluation only makes matters worse. It may be argued that the muse of poetry is indestructible and never fails to avenge the perversion of her purposes and the adulteration of her essence. Lydia Sigourney was arch-priestess of an order which had taken vows to prosperity, fatuity and sentiment. She blurred the outlines of the Evangelical scheme of thought and softened its severities while retaining its direct appeal to the emotional surfaces. She made it possible for her audience to love, to suffer, to act and to die vicariously and at no personal inconvenience while lounging in a hammock or warming the feet by the fire. She echoed the opinions of her readers and flattered their egos. What Lydia Sigourney said was exactly what they thought. To a generation emerging into the comfortable materialism of the nineteenth century she was balm to the nerves and a sedative to the conscience. She restated and justified every platitude that the era had coined for its comfort.

Mrs. Sigourney — this was the name by which her doting public knew her — was born in Norwich, Connecticut, in 1791, the daughter of Ezekiel Howard, the chief gardener of Madam Daniel Lathrop, the relict of a prosperous physician. Lydia was the child of her father's second marriage, named for his first wife. Ezekiel Howard had served in the Revolutionary War and was a dour and an elderly husband to Lydia's young schoolteacher mother. He held, from the point of view of his gifted daughter, a most advantageous job. As chief gardener he lived on Madam Lathrop's estate and was able to offer to pretty little Lydia the run of the garden, from the confines of which she strayed by easy stages into the house. Here Lydia became a rover at will in Madam Lathrop's library. With a quickness of perception astonishing in one so young, she successfully captivated the lonely Madam Lathrop by the display of a thousand winning ways and an affection that was little short of obsessive.

Like her contemporary and English counterpart, Felicia Dorothea Brown Hemans, she was precocious, and before

LYDIA HUNTLEY SIGOURNEY

From an engraving by A. H. Ritchie for the
American Literary Magazine
Courtesy of the Boston Athenaeum

"a Connecticut Yankee, gone astray among the muses"
(*page 72*)

she had entered her teens she had fitted in a good deal of indiscriminate reading. Mrs. Hemans, the future author of "The boy stood on the burning deck," lodged herself in an apple tree at the age of six to read Shakespeare, presenting, according to William Michael Rosetti, "A pretty picture [that] . . . would not be unworthy of realization by art." We must suppose that an equally pretty picture, suitable for framing, must have been presented by little Lydia Howard, pushing back her rich curls from her brow as she worked her way through the Poets in the pleasing atmosphere of Madam Lathrop's premises.

The fine houses of the Connecticut River Valley abounded in oriental carpets and eggshell porcelain, in crewel-work bedspreads and family plate. Gentlemen dined off dishes designed especially for them in China — the twelve disciples, Pontius Pilate giving judgment, Paul preaching to the Romans, all furnished with slanting eyes, gazed inscrutably from the recesses of soup tureens and the surfaces of dinnerware. Not even Calvinism could quell the exuberance of the river valley. It was ordained rich. Washington College (subsequently Trinity) was Episcopal. The green pastures, the still waters, the natural wealth that bred commerce and prosperity softened and sweetened the austere lives of the Puritan settlers. Their descendants lived in luxury and beauty. Elegant mansions commanded sweeping views of the green hills and the shining river: stately churches thrust their white steeples pranked with goldleaf over the treetops. Their naves were wide-windowed and lashed with sunlight, their porches embowered in lilac and althea. It was not difficult for young Lydia to acquire a taste for the finer things. But being a practical girl as well as a pretty and poetic one, Lydia was prepared to work for what she wanted. Whatever else may be stated to her disadvantage, it can never be said that she was lazy. She maintained an attitude of uncompromising devotion to Madam Lathrop that would have exhausted the powers of a feebler nature and was not the less remarkable for being as intense as it was sentimental. Lydia was not, however, required by fate to hold one pose indefinitely. When the girl was about fourteen Madam Lathrop died. This event, which could have surprised nobody, since the old lady had long been in her dotage, was just the background which the sensitive Lydia needed for the public display of her capacities. She indulged in such transports of grief that the whole town of Norwich was struck dumb with admiration. She sobbed, she swooned, she sickened. At Madam Lathrop's funeral she appeared to be taken with a fit and stared fixedly before her until removed by kindly hands to a place where she might revel privately in her sorrows. But in Lydia's opinion privacy was no place in which to suffer the loss of a dear old lady. She took to poetry and described the funeral and herself — herself especially — in terms of remorseless tenderness. "And sickening on her lowly tomb the broken floweret lay," she lamented while glancing sharply around, as broken flowerets do, for another patron.

Lydia's anguish paid off handsomely, and one rich old lady led quickly to another. Madam Lathrop had moved, when inhabiting this vale of tears, in circles which included the Wadsworths of Hartford, a family that commanded an extensive post-Revolutionary fortune. Lydia's avalanche of woe over the demise of Madam Lathrop impressed Madam Wadsworth most favorably and from Madam Wadsworth's good books it was an easy step to those of her son, Daniel. The river valley was just then in need of a Maecenas. Daniel Wadsworth was a rich bachelor with time on his hands: he slipped into the role of general patron from Windsor Locks to Norwich and his generosity set Lydia's feet on the straight and primrose path to fame.

Under Daniel Wadsworth's benign influence Lydia addressed herself to publication in 1815 and had no sooner committed words to paper than *Moral Pieces in Prose and Verse* was given to the world. The book found readers at once and was quickly followed by a second. The volumes dealt in catchpenny phrases already made familiar by Lydia's predecessors, but they had the merit of being easily grasped and people could apply them readily to their own dilemmas. Lydia could think of no more compelling adjective to attach to a hedgerow than to state categorically that it was verdant, a declaration that cannot be gainsaid although it does nothing for the hedgerow. Lydia in fact did nothing for anything, and the success of this maneuver must be measured by the popularity which rewarded it.

Her audience, bred on the *Cheap Repository Tracts* and *The Shepherd of Salisbury Plain* (Mrs. More's popularity in America was by no means slight — she boasted of "many American visitors"), was delighted to find that the United States could produce more of the same. Here was the same collection of lofty sentiments, here was the same unimpeachable piety but the scene was home. Lydia

hymned deathbeds, hoary locks, humble worth, nature —
most of the familiar garden plants were apostrophized
— and the animal kingdom. Nor was she a stranger to
patriotic sentiment. The Founding Fathers were all afflicted
with gawky verses, flung at their marble feet as fast as
words gushed from the pen. Living statesmen were pelted
with the same paper shower. It did not matter either to the
author or to the general reader that Mrs. Sigourney's
poems were more often than not the same one rearranged
to suit the subject. The mere sight of a state capitol reduced
her to instant verse. "Hail holy dome!" she wrote; many
of Lydia's poems began with "Hail," or alternatively "Ho,"
and she could never resist a dome. She could not even
resist a stone wall. When she visited the Beechers at their
family farm, "Nutplains," the spectacle of Lydia's raptures
on perceiving the dry wall at the end of the lawn made their
hospitality its own reward. "Oh ye muted ramparts!"
declaimed Lydia, clasping her hands and providing the
Beechers with a vision of Mrs. Sigourney at work that
lasted even unto the third generation.

Lydia Howard could not of course rely solely on her pen
for support at the beginning of her career. In spite of the
patronage of Daniel Wadsworth she had a way to make
and aged parents to support. Lydia's mother was only
forty-three at the time that her daughter took to describing
her forebears in these terms and might have found the
classification objectionable, but since aged parents were
desirable equipment for a poetess Mrs. Howard was forced
to submit to being one. With her customary devotion to
duty Lydia sought gainful employment and turned school-

teacher. Adaptable and quick-witted she never attacked any task without results. She succeeded in opening her own Select Seminary for Young Ladies in Hartford in 1814 after teaching for two years in Norwich.

Lydia's school predated the movement for serious female education by some years. Catharine Beecher's Hartford Female Seminary, which embodied the notion that girls should partake of some of the mental disciplines imposed upon their brothers, was not founded until after Lydia had left her school in order to marry. Lydia's institution in no way advanced the cause of higher learning. Canon Mozley's comments on the Evangelical movement at St. Edmunds Hall, Oxford, could have been applied to the state of education at Lydia's Select Seminary:

> *Their knowledge was imaginary. So too was their introspection, their futures, sometimes even their past . . . The quick ripening mind, for lack of other matters feeds upon itself . . . These [young people] had been reared on insubstantial and stimulating good; on pious tales, on high-wrought death-beds, on conversations as they ought to be, on one-sided biographies. Truth of opinion, they had always been told, was incomparably more important than truth of fact.*

Lydia's pupils were taught that the earth was created in six days about two thousand years before the birth of Christ. They learned useful moral lessons from the works of Mrs. More and other popular writers. They prayed, sang hymns, embroidered and captured a few words of French for exhibition purposes. Their education, in short, suited them to be in later life Lydia's vast uncritical audience to whom, as Geraldine Jewsbury said of Mrs. Hemans, "anything abstract or scientific was unintelligible and distasteful."

Lydia's teaching years came to an end in 1819 when after one or two misapplications her affections came to rest on Mr. Charles Sigourney of Hartford, a widower, some years older than his bride, with two young children. Mr. Sigourney was a prosperous hardware merchant and at the time of his second marriage was apparently enough of a skinflint to ensure pretty effectively that he would remain prosperous. Lydia, still young and full of vitality, showered on him a cascade of affection that was quite unjustified by any qualities of his. He was a man of ordinary capacities and a great deal of conceit who had been born into comfortable circumstances and fancied himself a patrician. Lydia idealized the thin-lipped little Yankee merchant who resembled a featherless owl into a nobleman who had conferred inestimable honor on a humble but adoring bride. It never seemed to occur to her that she was his superior in energy and even in attainment. She persisted in the legend that he was handsome, brilliant, generous and brave and never publicly swerved from her story in the face of her husband's pettiness, incompetence and incapacity for warmth or tenderness.

In due course the Sigourneys produced two more children, a daughter and a son, and acquired an imposing house with grounds to match. Expenses soared. The fact of the matter was that in spite of Mr. Sigourney's pretensions to pedigree and the commercial eminence which he occupied as president of the Phoenix Bank, Trustee of Washington

College and Warden of Christ Church, his ventures did not prosper. He was honest and conscientious but he was also vain, sour, stingy and rigidly attached to his own view of himself as something above the common lot. Egotistical, unpopular and not particularly astute, he lacked the New Englander's gift for turning one dollar into two. A house and grounds, a growing family and a position in society are not maintained on mere thrift, and it soon became obvious that the Sigourney family was to depend largely on Lydia. Lydia was clever and when necessity drove could be frugal. She could transform a cast-off petticoat into a pair of Sunday trousers for a small boy and fill the larder with pies of her own baking; but the family needed more money so Lydia took up her trusty pen. Mr. Sigourney, in spite of the advantages which this gesture promised, viewed his wife's career as a threat. His aristocratic privacy stood in danger of being subjected to publicity for which he had a noble distaste. His pride was in jeopardy. Lydia, to humor him, submitted at first to anonymity. Her publishers objected. Readers would be more willing to mingle their tears with those of a Mrs. Sigourney than with some unknown "lady" over "The deaths of infants, dying boys' last bequests, the death of consumptive girls, of missionaries in Burma and Liberia, of poets, lunatics, artists and sailors, college students and deaf, dumb and blind girls," as Gordon Haight has described the contents of many of her volumes.

Mr. Sigourney in his own interests and to soothe his wife's clamoring public had ultimately to give in, which he did with no very good grace. His wife was a public figure and his noble name, through no merit of his, was a household word. The situation did not make for family happiness. The Sigourneys bickered, the children were fretful and rebellious, inclined to squirm or resort to mute, embarrassed protest against the rising tide of their mother's fame, while Lydia advised other quarrelsome families that, "if there is a spot on earth which angels might long to visit and where they might fondly linger, it is the loving Christian family."

Elsewhere Lydia had moments of cautious honesty. None of her stories contain character sketches or anything else that might remotely be construed as autobiographical, but she permitted herself an occasional comment that could as well have been applied to her own drab married life as to that of the unhappy wives in her stories.

In *The Intemperate*, for example, a tractarian novelette on the downfall of a drunkard, an occasional moment of truth crops up in the welter of words that served Mrs. Sigourney for a style. "There is no tyranny so perfect as that of a capricious and alienated husband," she declares. The short sentence stands out from its elaborate fellows sudden as a cricket call. The reader is forced to sympathize with the abused and neglected wife. "As a woman forsaken and grieved in spirit, and as a wife of youth when thou wast refused, I have called thee, saith thy God," cries Lydia Sigourney and for a moment we believe what she has to say. A century ago thousands of lonely housewives nodded in agreement and read on to see what happened next. For, like Hannah More, in her stories Lydia knew how to carry her reader from page to page. Her language is inflated, her feeling is false, her characters are sawdust and we read on anyway because she tells a story. Readers will endure anything for a story and will endure nothing without it. *The Shepherd of Salisbury Plain, The Intemperate* and Mrs. Aphra Behn's *Oroonoko* are stories, and in their day they were spellbinders. It is questionable whether any drinker stayed away from his drink because of reading *The Intemperate*, but Mrs. Sigourney's sales figures justify the conjecture that drinkers and nondrinkers alike read the tale from cover to cover.

And in order that the "capricious and alienated husband" should want for nothing, Lydia's output from 1822 onward was little short of torrential. Poems, stories, moral reflections spurted like blood from an artery. In 1833 she wrote more than a thousand pages. In 1836 when Edgar Allan Poe's "Israfel" lay buried in its middle section, the *Southern Literary Messenger* bore Lydia's name like a talisman and advertised a poem of hers as a main feature. Louis Godey paid her five hundred dollars for the privilege of carrying her name even without a contribution in his *Lady's Book*.

There was no subject too exalted or too mere for her consideration. In tones that would have done credit to the awful Mrs. More herself, Lydia admonished the whores and fences who languished in the female penitentiary at Wethersfield.

> *The way of wickedness is hard,*
> *Its bitter fruits we know.*
> *Shame in the world is its reward*
> *And in the future woe.*

Napoleon Bonaparte fared no better and at much greater length. His poem begins with "Ho" rather than "Hail." It bears comparison with Hannah More's effusions on

slavery and stands as an instance of the grand manner.
Lydia wrote many grand poems but "The Return of
Napoleon from St. Helena" is compact of grandeur. It
has the peculiar and pompous charm of a Victorian relic,
an umbrella stand or an aspidistra on a whatnot.

> *Ho! City of the Gay!*
> *Paris, what festal rite*
> *Doth call thy thronging millions forth*
> *All eager for the sight?*
> *Thy soldiers line the streets*
> *In fixed and stern array*
> *With buckled helm and bayonet*
> *As on the battle day.*

After fourteen stanzas of this kind of thing, the poem
concludes on a note of stern disapproval:

> *Mysterious one and proud,*
> *In the land where shadows reign,*
> *Hast thou met the flocking ghosts of those*
> *Who at thy nod were slain?*
> *Oh when the cry of that spectral host*
> *Like a rushing blast shall be*
> *What will thy answer be to them?*
> *And what thy God's to thee?*

It cannot truthfully be said that Napoleon's interment
is Mrs. Sigourney's best poem. On the other hand it is
scarcely her worst. It is in fact an excellent example of a
bad poem. It enabled people at no extra effort to identify
themselves with a value judgment on Napoleon, congratu-
late themselves, nod and read on.

Dissatisfied in spite of the ever-expanding size of her

public, Lydia saw to it that copies of her work were sent to every great name on the American continent and to many beyond the seas. In fact, her financial position suffered owing to the reckless generosity with which she offered presentation copies of her works. The Great, depending on their temperaments, either acknowledged with varying degrees of courtesy her persistent attentions or ignored them. Ralph Waldo Emerson succeeded in carrying on as though she did not exist. Edgar Allan Poe, blinded apparently by her inflated reputation and aware that her name was a passport to heavy sales whenever it appeared in a magazine, courted her favor and objected on patriotic grounds to her being described as "the American Mrs. Hemans." Was it not good enough to be Mrs. Sigourney? She was as flowery, portentous and prolific as Mrs. Hemans in her own right. Readers and publishers could never have enough of coffined children, broken flowerets and hoary locks. Lydia had a special regard for an advanced degree of senility and her raptures on this subject never lost their eloquence or their market value.

Mrs. Sigourney was not one however to waste her forces forever on the domestic and the personal. She tackled Napoleon, she tackled Columbus and she had early made the red man her prey. She wrote *Traits of the Aborigines of America* and she wrote an epic on Pocahontas in balky eight-line stanzas charged with splendid sentiments and barbarians falling victim to Christianity. Lydia's language for the Indian was biblical, full of ye's and 'tis's and other archaisms, as well as metaphors with a tendency to lurch out of control.

Ye say, they all have passed away,
That noble race and brave;
That their light canoes have vanished
From off the crested wave;
That, 'mid the forest where they roamed,
There rings no hunter's shout;
But their name is on your waters, —
*Ye may not wash it out.**

Mrs. Sigourney's verse has one extraordinary quality. As poetry it fails in every respect. It does not challenge the imagination or stir the emotions or enflame the curiosity. But one is aware — just around the corner, as it were — of a haunting tendency to arouse mirth. It is as though the phosphorescent bones of a comic talent lay buried beneath the faded stage properties of her content, lambent in the idiosyncrasies of her diction — something not to be analyzed but merely sensed, like the musk of a skunk after rain. After plodding through volumes of intolerable stuff we find ourselves laughing, not at something so obvious as a mixed metaphor of waters from which we may not wash out names, but at accidents much more subtle. They have almost the quality of art. Anapests lope in where dactyls fear to tread. Some quirk of emphasis, some misplaced alliteration, some misalliance between image and allegory appear upon the page to lure us into laughter. Let us look at Lydia's lines to a pelican. It is possible presumably to perpetrate a poem to a pelican, although for some reason or other a pelican makes a somewhat unwieldy subject, less manageable, say, than a wingèd horse. Pelicans

---

* From "Indian Names."

fall into the same category as kangaroos and penguins and must be tackled sideways rather than straight on, or at least from some slightly different angle than that appropriate to lions or nightingales or Spartan soldiers or unrequited love. Edward Lear dealt fearlessly and thoroughly with pelicans. They waddle through his delightful poem, singing choruses and are pleasant and believable which is all that we require of a pelican. Mrs. Sigourney required more. For her the pelican is the exemplar of the soul. The pelican, like the soul, is flapping out to sea. Instances of the soul flapping out to sea like a pelican are rare in English verse. The pelican does not really remind us of the soul. But for Lydia the pelican assumed this questionable shape, or rather she forced the assumption on it, which is not quite the same thing, and came up with the following results:

> *Then shall the soul enslaved no more*
> *Launch calmly on Salvation's sea*
> *And part from time's receding shore,*
> *Lone, peaceful pelican, like thee.*

It is the last line that turns the trick. Something clowns in the four-foot verse and in the arrangement of stresses. It is correct and absurd. It resembles Mrs. Sigourney's defense of maize as a proper subject for poetic comment. Why not maize indeed? Except when it is described as "that stately vegetable" we are disinclined to take an ear of corn seriously. It is better considered as something to eat off a cob or pop over a fire and we tend to disbelieve in its innate stateliness.

When poor Lydia turned her distinguished attention to

conscious humor the worst happened. She could never be funny on purpose. When she wrote about brooms and dusters they turned out to be no more amusing than brooms and dusters usually are, and when she wrote a mock ode to a goose she succeeded in being merely impertinent.

For, effective and warmhearted as Lydia Sigourney was, she was in no position to patronize geese. She proceeded through life like a goose — a kindly and even clever goose — but nonetheless gracelessly and aggressively. She sighed and sentimentalized over her miserly and unsympathetic husband and when all the fire of her affection for him was doused she turned a similar spotlight on her children. She dramatized and publicized them before they finally escaped, or as in the case of the younger, died. He died lingeringly and distressingly of tuberculosis. His mother, with whom he did not get along, and on whose account he clearly suffered agonies of embarrassment, nursed him faithfully, keeping up a running commentary on the progress of his disease for the edification of all who would listen. No miserable detail of the sickroom remained unrecounted until the poor boy found refuge in the grave. What her real emotions were toward her sad, uncommunicative son she probably would have been the last to know. She dilated upon his death in the same rococo terms which she used to describe the death of the daughter in her narrative *The Father*, and all the fustian language employed in the story was put to the service of the real event.

Lydia Sigourney met bereavement with a theatrical gesture; slights and closed doors with reiterated appeals for notice and louder rattlings of the doorknob. She was shameless, innocent and, it would seem, a stranger to physical fear. On the return journey from her trip to England and the Continent, the vessel on which she traveled encountered a number of icebergs in a fog off the coast of England. The danger was acute. The captain had no choice but to steer the ship through the floes and hope that no unseen spur would shipwreck him at any moment. President Wayland of Brown University retired to his cabin to pray. The other passengers, aware that their last hour might be upon them, followed his example, all except Lydia Sigourney. She remained on deck, deriving inspiration from the sight of the great prow-splitters gliding toward the ship in the misty moonlight and coolly taking notes.

Lydia viewed Europe as she viewed stone walls, state capitol domes, female prisoners, pelicans and Napoleon — with hail's and ho's. She saw Paris, London, cathedrals, crowned heads, the Lake Country, Miss Maria Edgeworth, Mrs. Southey, Samuel Rogers and, heaven help us, Thomas Carlyle. There is something almost endearing about the figure of Lydia as she emerges against the background of Europe. She had planned and longed for the journey. She made it at last in middle age. She constituted the archetypal burlesque of the Innocent Abroad, frisking through historic sites, annoying people with her good-natured impertinence and having a perfectly lovely time. Royalty received her. She wrote an effusion on the uncorseted figure of Queen Marie Amélie, the inoffensive spouse of Louis Philippe, dwelling complacently on the simplicity of the Queen's dress and calling on American women to follow this august example, and, in so many words, dispense with the whale-bone. The King and Queen received Mrs. Sigourney with their usual democratic aplomb. It is impossible not to believe that an unspoken affinity must have existed between two such inveterate gallery players as Louis Philippe and Lydia. He remarked to her with amiable condescension that America was very large. She agreed that it was. There was a further reference to Niagara Falls before His Majesty passed on to the next visitor. Mrs. Sigourney chose the first opportunity to see that the King and Queen received copies of her work and they retaliated with a diamond bracelet. The bracelet thereafter figured largely in Lydia's conversation. Legends sprang up around it. It was plucked from the Queen's wrist and presented to Lydia personally on the spot like a decoration on the field of battle; alterna-tively it was not given by Queen Marie Amélie but by Queen Victoria herself.

The visit to England was less peaceful than the one to France. The natives were not separated from Lydia by the language barrier and few of them were equipped to deal with her brand of highhearted aggression. William Wordsworth was an easy mark and his hoary locks forth-with fell afoul of a poem.

The Carlyles endured a visit. Jane Welsh Carlyle had little use for Americans as it was. She would gladly, as she said, have taken a poker to most of them. A mistress of the total snub she was capable of sitting through any conversation, answering impudent questions in the barest monosyllables. But after being importuned the "lion's wife" gave in and let Lydia come to tea. She came, bringing two uninvited fellow Yankees to a meal which that day included the Wedgwoods, the Darwins, and the Carlyles' friend Julia Smith. Mrs. Carlyle afterwards gave vent to her feelings: "This figure of an over-the-water poetess, be-plastered with rouge and pomatum, bare-necked at an age which had left certainty far behind." Lydia's two acquaintances added insult to injury: "the male in an embroidered satin waistcoat," the female "with a gold tiara."

The party was a disaster. The Americans stared and simpered. The intervals of silence between remarks were prolonged for minutes together. The "lion" was understandably surly. Lydia viewed the infuriated company as calmly as she was later to view the icebergs. She had come to England to see, among other items of interest, Thomas Carlyle. She saw him and she evidently did not require that he should be agreeable. All that she asked was that he exist — like Stonehenge. Having seen him, she came away well satisfied and apparently unconscious of having either given or received an outrage.

To offset the Carlyles the second Mrs. Robert Southey welcomed the approaches of the lively American visitor with much more enthusiasm than discretion warranted. Here all Lydia's proclivities were called into play. She had barely crossed the threshold of the poor mad poet's house than she was the recipient of Mrs. Southey's confidence on a scale which must have satisfied even Lydia Sigourney's voracity for scenes of domestic sorrow. Robert Southey was insane. His wife was living in seclusion, with little companionship and nobody in whom to confide the details of what must have been an almost intolerable existence. The sympathetic foreigner called out disclosures both in conversation and in subsequent letters that would never have seen daylight had Mrs. Southey had an inkling that Mrs. Sigourney would make every syllable public on her return to the United States.

Lydia paraded Mrs. Southey's misery and exaggerated the dimensions of the friendship until the victim protested vigorously. Lydia ignored the protests as long as possible and then vented her injured feelings by constant glowing references to Southey's first wife, long dead, all but ignoring the existence of the second. Frightened by this episode, other potential victims, such as Miss Edgeworth, who had unwisely slipped into correspondence with Lydia, began to clutch their skirts about them. Maria Edgeworth put her foot down, gently but firmly, at Lydia's repeated requests for permission to quote directly from the letters which the Irish writer had been unguarded enough to write her. Miss Edgeworth approved of Lydia Sigourney and even liked her but she would not permit so much as a comma of her private correspondence to be published. Lydia besought her in vain. To Mrs. Sigourney's last begging letter Miss Edgeworth returned no answer and there the friendship ended.

Lydia was happiest in her relations with Samuel Rogers, a banker, a poet and an Evangelical. Rogers had an inexhaustible supply of sentiment, and he engaged in an elderly flirtation with Lydia which afforded them both enjoyment without risk. This relationship was permanent and unclouded and must have done much to console Mrs.

Sigourney for the loss of Mrs. Southey and Miss Edge-worth.

Lydia's long and industrious life ended with one small disappointment. Her native city of Norwich failed to recognize the merits of this special child and showed a rather churlish disposition to ignore her. The town where she had lived most of her life displayed more courtesy, and Sigourney Street remains a memorial to the Sweet Singer of Hartford. Mrs. Sigourney's last years were spent blame-lessly in charitable works, in the enjoyment of a reputation earned by unfailing hard work and in lively discourse with her neighbors and friends. She was generous and sympa-thetic to children, black as well as white, kind to animals and old people, an elderly lady of whom people had grown fond, whose indiscretions were of no importance and whose days of triumph were already a memory. She died in 1865 and her friends in Hartford mourned her sincerely. She had given the world a great deal of harmless entertainment. For forty-five years she had obediently supplied a large public with exactly what it required. She belongs not to a culture but to a state of mind, the state of mind of her readers. She shared and expressed their thoughts and opinions. The art of fiction made the message of the Evangelicals palatable and habit-forming. Mrs. Sigourney merely took advantage of the habit and added extra flavor-ing to the dose while extracting most of its basic ingredients. Her audience wanted easy solutions and happy endings. Sin was to be punished as a matter of course but the public was more concerned to see virtue rewarded. It was a public with a will and a loud voice, a largely feminine public which wanted total abstinence, Sunday observance and domestic affections. It did not take kindly to criticism. The writers whom it clasped to its bosom shared its prejudices. Mrs. Hemans retired to her bed when her work was noticed unfavorably. Mrs. Sigourney was so wounded by the mere rumor that Poe had dealt with her severely in his review of *Zinzendorf, and Other Poems* that she sulked in her tent until he actually made amends. He was trying to make the publications of which he was editor at various times pay their way and, like Louis Godey, he was frantic to name her among his contributors. "That we have evinced any severity amounting to unkindness is an accusation of which you will, I hope, unhesitatingly acquit us," he cajoled. The soothing tones worked and he was rewarded with a contribution.

It is something of a puzzle that Poe, who could so ruthlessly trample on William Ellery Channing, found Mrs. Sigourney not only endurable but even significant. He could take her seriously while admitting in her certain faults just as William Michael Rossetti could take Mrs. Hemans seriously. "The atmosphere of her verse," wrote Rossetti of Mrs. Hemans, "is by no means bracing. It is not only feminine but female poetry. Besides exhibiting the fineness and charm of womanhood it has the monotone of mere sex. . . . Mrs. Hemans has that love of the good and horror of evil which characterize a scrupulous female mind and which we may most rightly praise without concluding that they favor poetical robustness, or even perfection in literary form."

Critics and poets may roar with the pain of it all but

poetry suffers no real harm at the hands of Lydia Sigourney, or for that matter from any of the scribbling sisterhood from Mrs. More on down. Literature survives them as the Victory of Samothrace survives plaster-of-Paris statuettes and bronze deer on front lawns. Lydia molders in the literary attic, smelling of mice and mothballs, among the stuffed birds, the keys that no longer fit our locks, the odd bits of chipped porcelain, the quaint clothing and the bundle of letters almost too faded to read. They are impermanent things but they shape the past for us in small ways. Through them we know how our obscure ancestors lived their daily lives. The Gettysburg Address, *Leaves of Grass*, the lyric poems of Ralph Waldo Emerson may tell us something of the genius of the age, but we can learn nothing from them of how people whiled away a rainy summer Sunday in the middle of the nineteenth century. If we wish to know how this was done we turn to Lydia Sigourney. As we riffle the pages of a fat little volume we can for a moment fancy ourselves, rather tightly laced, sitting in a curtained parlor in a high-ceilinged house, one of many such houses that stand in the shady streets of Hartford, Connecticut, about the year 1858. Rosewood piano and dark furniture smelling of linseed oil. Morning sermon and the ritual of lunch already forgotten. Evening prayers to come. Monday morning with the coppers full of clothing to be washed looming ahead. We dip into *Moral Pieces in Prose and Verse* or *The Young Ladies Offering of Gems of Prose and Poetry* (containing seven touching stories by Mrs. Sigourney) while the rain patters monotonously on the roof. We have given up on that rather formidable publication, *The Atlantic Monthly*, whose contents have merely confused us. In any case that kind of thing never lasts. The rain weeps down the windowpane and there is a distant roll of thunder to the south of us. It is a dull Sunday, like most Sundays. But Mrs. Sigourney eases it on its way to the work-a-day week. As we read, everything becomes a little unreal. We are lifted out of ourselves and we weep with genuine enjoyment over deaths that do not affect us and adventures that cannot dismay. Mrs. Sigourney alters nothing. She is merely a respite. Everything is exactly as it should be. The bad are very bad, the good are very good. Everything turns out as we thought it would. There are no shocks. We weep along happily, turning page after page to see what happens next.

Literature gains nothing from Mrs. Sigourney's sixty-odd volumes but history would miss her if she had never existed. As much a sign of her time as the horsehair sofa on which her avid reader sits, she flounces through the fringes of the era, curls gleaming, petticoats a-swish, articulate and industrious, shedding tears, baking pies, making money, a Connecticut Yankee, gone astray among the muses, but undaunted and determined to make the most of the adventure.

MISS BEECHER IN HELL

M ANY TIMES by the presentation of such an awful
theme (THE ETERNAL IRREMEDIABLE LOSS OF THE
SOUL), I have brought the young to me with tears and
willing docility, and to the question 'What can we do to
be saved?' my shut-up heart was ready to exclaim 'Nothing!' . . . I have been so burdened [as] to take every
lawful mode to turn my thoughts to other less exciting
themes."

The eternal irremediable loss of the soul is a theme
whose excitement can scarcely be overestimated and this
was something that Catharine Esther Beecher, the author
of the somewhat disheveled paragraph quoted above, was
not likely to overlook.

"If the fear of the Lord," Catharine continues, "is the
beginning of wisdom, I certainly began aright." Catharine's
case was not an unusual one for her time and place: she
was a nineteenth-century Connecticut Congregationalist.
At the time of Catharine's birth the heroic drama of Congregationalism in the New World was reaching its epilogue.

The orthodox clergy mouthed their last strophes and anti-strophes from Holy Yale, while Unitarian Harvard hardly took the trouble to listen. Three revolutions, the American, the French and the Industrial, had remade the image of man and "the cold, mad, feary father" of the Puritans was forsaking the white temples to join Peor and Baalim in the land of forgotten gods. But when the gods go they go with a horrid clang, and the old fury clung to life like grim death. When Catharine Beecher was born in East-hampton, Long Island, in 1800 Jonathan Edwards was still angrily alive and very very dangerous.

"Oh thou little immortal!" exclaimed the promising young Congregationalist minister Lyman Beecher when the newborn Catharine, his first child, was laid in his arms. The greeting was as much a warning as a welcome, for this heritage of immortality was to a strict Calvinist as fissionable an endowment as a cargo of U-235. Before the squirming hour-old baby lay the two inescapable alternatives of eternity: unmitigated bliss or unspeakable never-ending torment, foreordained before the dawn of time and dependent on the whim of a maniacal paranoid whose only preoccupation lay in the gratification of his self-love. Having deprived man of the means to salvation this uncontrollable egotist then held him responsible for his failure to achieve it and as if this were not enough he then inflicted on the helpless soul and body unmentionable torture forever and ever. Even newborn infants were not exempt but fried with the rest that their punishment might show forth God's glory. The number of the "elect" was so negligible that their state, however blissful, scarcely merited consideration. It was not a comfortable doctrine.

In spite of the risks inherent in bringing children into the world Lyman Beecher never flinched from his duties as a begetter. Eleven little Beechers (the offspring of two of Beecher's three wives) followed Catharine into the world with an optimism that defies all reason in view of their father's beliefs. As it happened, neither the first nor the second Mrs. Lyman Beecher would put up with the damnation of infants. As a young minister, mouthing fire and brimstone, Lyman had courted Roxana Foote, an Episcopalian. He did not permit her to labor long under the pleasant delusions of the Anglican faith. He was no sooner betrothed than he began propounding to his love some of the more disquieting tenets of Calvinism, urging her to yield, like Mrs. Jonathan Edwards, "with sweet submission to the sovereign will of God, of being fully willing to die in horror and live a thousand years in horror — even to be eternally damned . . . if it be most to the glory of God." Roxana fell into such transports of alternating religious ecstasy and panic that her family "feared for her reason."

While the courtship proceeded in this satisfactory manner Lyman had reckoned without Roxana's logical powers. To be damned, she reasoned, implied that she must be utterly wicked and depraved: since it was out of the question that wickedness and depravity in her should redound to God's glory she was, *ergo*, not damned or about to be. This argument made sense and left a bad bruise on Lyman's orthodoxy from which he did not recover. He shook in his shoes but he married her and set his feet firmly on the path that led ultimately to his three trials for heresy.

Life in the Beecher parsonages (of which Lyman occu-

pied a number in and about New England during Catharine's childhood) with the steady arrival of immortals
year after year was evidently calculated to distract the
mind from the future state in an effort to keep up with
the demands of this one. Lyman was a devoted and energetic parent and the children were as red-cheeked, well
grown and inventive a quiverful as any parson could
desire. At an early age Catharine discovered that she
owned a remarkably handsome head of hair and she took
pains to dress and display it in and out of season, tossing
her curls for visitors and finding occasions to let them fall
in graceful tresses over the pages of her book if anyone
was by to see.

"My strict religious training," says Catharine in her
recollections of her childhood, "made little impression on
me for I never heard anything so dull and unintelligible."
Moral depravity in toddlers was apparently of epidemic
proportions, and *The Christian Spectator* comments glumly
on the situation in an article on Christian education: "The
aversion of the natural heart to religion is manifest from
the beginning. Children naturally dislike it and they are
not to be won over to its demands and to be modelled by
its rules without the most strenuous efforts." In Catharine's
case the efforts were not nearly strenuous enough; rather,
she lived for "doll dressing, baby house building, afterward
drawing, painting, snow-castles, forts, summer excursions,
school and family drama-acting and the like." *Don Quixote*
was much more to her mind than the pious dissertations
that stocked her father's library and she wondered as she
leafed through Reid's work on mental science "how people
could read such stuff." The enchanting little sister, Harriet

(the future Mrs. Stowe), with her unconquerable passion
for gaiety, kept the whole kindle in gales of laughter. She
was so clever, sighed Lyman, that he would have given a
hundred dollars to have had her born a boy, for she would
surely have made her mark.

But for all the combing of curls and the running up
of home theatricals this charming and gifted household
preserved its temporary happiness by ignoring the dragon
rather than fighting it. For whether they thought of it or
not, predestination and the doctrine of election were a
central fact of their lives, but, as Catharine says: "Since
the selection of the recipients of this favor [Grace] was
regulated by a divine decree of election . . . [and] it was
so merely as a matter of mere chance and there seemed so
little adaptation of means to ends that there was very little
motive of any kind to lead a religious life." Harriet at the
age of nine trifled with what struck her father's friend the
Reverend Joel Hawes of Hartford as a kind of wildcat
conversion. Delight in religion he assured the child, was
not to be mistaken for Grace, and mere love of God was
insufficient to salvation. Despite her charm and high spirits
Harriet learned the harsh realities of eternity early.

"Fearful to them were the shadows that lay over the
cradle and the grave," she tells us. "The mother clasped
her babe to her bosom and looked with shuddering to the
awful oncoming trial of free agency with its terrible
responsibilities and risks. . . . When the stroke of death
came and some young thoughtless head was laid suddenly
low, who can say what silent anguish of loving hearts
sounded the dread depths of eternity with the awful
question, 'Where?' "

For neither the prayers of the faithful, the intervention of the church, a godly life, nor the acts of redemption by the Saviour Himself availed the sinner in the hands of an angry God.

"Your wickedness makes you heavy as lead and you tend downward with great weight and pressure toward Hell. . . . God will be so far from pitying you when you cry to him that 'tis said he will only laugh and mock. . . . 'I will stain all my raiment with blood,'" whispers the mellifluous Edwards, corroborated by the terrible Samuel Hopkins: "The body can by omnipotence be made capable of suffering the greatest imaginable pain without producing dissolution or abating the least degree of life or sensibility. . . . One way in which God will show his power in punishing the wicked will be in strengthening and upholding their bodies and souls in torments which otherwise would have been intolerable."

How the old Moloch tore and rampaged! In his perpetual tantrum, unpropitiated and unpropitiable, he ravened after Rachel's children and observed the Crucifixion in a state of "calm, unmingled bliss," momentarily appeased by the spectacle of three hours' agony on the Cross. No misstep was too absurd for the violence of his consideration nor was any virtue sufficiently monstrous to placate his voracious ill temper. That he was only an archaic image, trapped in a gigantic Newtonian metaphor, could not concern the majority of his votaries. In the drab context of their daily lives he lived vivid as blood, omnipresent as air and playfully cruel as an Indian.

"And you children that are unconverted, don't you know that you are going down to Hell to bear the wrath of that

God that is now angry with you every day and night?"
continues Edwards, offering a word of warning to the
nursery. "Will you be the children of the devil when so
many children in the land are converted and are become
the holy happy children of the King of Kings?"

"The sermons preached by President Edwards," says
Harriet, ". . . are so terrific in their refined poetry of
torture that few persons of . . . sensibility could read
them without agony: and when . . . in those calm and
tender tones which never rose to passionate annunciation
he read these discourses the house was often filled with
shrieks and wailings . . . and [it is said] a brother minister
once laid hold of his skirts, exclaiming as in involuntary
agony, 'Oh, Mr. Edwards! Mr. Edwards! Is God not a
God of Mercy?' "

How merciful he was the great preacher took pains to
inform the fellow minister: "The saints will be sensible of
how great their salvation is . . . in the difference between
themselves who were by nature and perhaps by practice
no more sinful and ill deserving than they. Every time
they look upon the damned it will excite in them a lively
and admiring sense in the Grace of God in making them
so to differ. A view of the miseries of the damned will
double the ardor of the love and gratitude of the saints
in Heaven."

"Thus it happened," concludes Harriet in her remarks
on the New England sermon, "that while strong spirits
walked palm-crowned with victorious hymns along those
sublime paths, feebler and more sensitive ones lay along
the track, bleeding away in lifelong despair."

When Catharine was sixteen Roxana died, leaving the

young girl anxiously presiding over the younger children and attempting to comfort the heartbroken Lyman. She mourned her mother sincerely but she was at an age when no hardship could down her. Her natural health and spirits would assert themselves: "I was so happy that I could not do anything but enjoy life." Here was a sure indication of an unregenerate heart. Nothing short of total catastrophe would do her any good.

"Dear child," exclaimed Lyman in tears, "must I die too?" Catharine fobbed him off with a gratifying display of her own tears and put the matter out of her mind. She had her hands full with the cooking, clothing and education of the children; and about this time Lyman, instead of dying, went courting and the parsonage at Litchfield, Connecticut, prepared itself for a new mistress after two years of interregnum by Catharine.

Lyman's choice had fallen on Harriet King Porter, a woman as attractive and independent in her own way as Roxana. It was his fate to attach himself at all times to women who loved him dearly but had no use for his opinions. He never succeeded in converting either a wife or a daughter to his way of thinking. They found his ideas both impractical and unpleasant. They comforted his bed, mended his socks, kept his accounts, cooked his meals, waited on him hand and foot and solved their theological disputes with him by changing his religion for him as they changed the diapers on the baby. His defeat at the hands of Roxana had been significant, and Harriet lost no time in consolidating Roxana's gains. Lyman had no sooner installed his new wife in the parlor than he seized the opportunity to read her Edwards' *Sinners in the Hands of an Angry God*. Mrs. Beecher listened patiently for some minutes, then rose suddenly from her chair with a splendid swish of bridal petticoats: "Dr. Beecher, I shall not listen to another word of that slander on my Heavenly Father!" she exclaimed and swept from the room, leaving Lyman alone with his God.

Catharine welcomed the new mother with evident relief. Mrs. Beecher found her eldest stepdaughter a highly agreeable young woman with more than ordinary attainments: "a fine looking girl . . . not handsome, yet there is hardly anyone who appears better. . . ." It was just the moment for someone to love Catharine, and someone did. Alexander Metcalf Fisher, professor of mathematics and natural philosophy (now called physics) at Yale University, sought her hand in marriage. Born in 1794, Fisher seems to have been one of those Mozartean people whose lives, too soon ended, are a promise broken to a whole generation. Contemporary panegyrics on the young man read with all the spuriousness which such accounts usually convey but the structure, visible behind the ornamental adjectives, is startling in its strength and beauty. No human activity seemed beyond his scope. At the age of ten he threw away his arithmetic book and wrote himself a better one. At fourteen he entered Yale and graduated at the head of his class in 1813. When he was twenty-three the university appointed him adjunct professor of mathematics, and he became a full professor at twenty-five.

According to James Luce Kingsley, an older colleague, Fisher "had reached the limits which hitherto had bounded the fields of discovery. . . . [He had] an almost intuitive apprehension of truth in the exact sciences [and] . . . for the detection of error in the mazes of metaphysical speculation and for the quick perception of the ridiculous in human character, the follies and vices of which he had the power to expose with playful humor or the severity of satire."

Alexander Metcalf Fisher, the eldest son of a farmer of Franklin, Massachusetts, explored the theory of frequency modulation and did an accomplished monograph on the mathematical relationships contained within the diatonic scale, was fluent in Greek, Latin, Hebrew and French and entertained himself by writing science fiction. *A Journey to the Moon and Some of the Other Planets* is only less revealing of the exquisite quality of his intellect than his delicate diagrams for his computations of the eclipse of the sun on August 27, 1821.

As a traveler from "a small dull star just north of Aldebaran," Fisher describes deviations in the law of gravity and the variations in units of time to be expected on a voyage to outer space. The inhabitants of the distant asteroids he found infinitely superior to human beings in every respect, and they regarded him with a kindly disapproval while according him excellent treatment. They looked upon him "much as we do upon a stranger from the south seas" and were scandalized by his table manners. Their libraries and universities beggared description. The acquisition of knowledge was made simple by a common language; verse was free since "a poet would no more confide his poetry to the limitations of rhyme than a philosopher would allow

CATHARINE ESTHER BEECHER

A daguerreotype. Courtesy of the Women's Archives,
Radcliffe College, Cambridge, Massachusetts

*"a fine looking girl . . . not handsome, yet there is hardly
anyone who appears better. . . ." (page 81)*

ALEXANDER METCALF FISHER

From a portrait by Samuel Finley Breese Morse
Courtesy of the Yale University Art Gallery

"Hamlet-like in his academic robes" (*page 83*)

himself to be constricted by the margins of a page." It was a joyous journey.

His personal endowments (incredible to relate) were of as high a quality as his intellectual parts. Samuel Finley Breese Morse painted a portrait of him after his death from a series of sketches and even his family found it a good likeness. He sits wrapped Hamlet-like in his academic robes; his features are finely formed, dark hair curls above a noble forehead; in one slim hand he holds a pen. Behind him a swollen sea and a storm in dramatic chiaroscuro set off his pensive and melancholy good looks to imperial advantage. To this exhausting catalogue of perfections Fisher added "a deep sense of religious obligation. Few have manifested a higher reverence for the divine law or failed less in their obedience to the precepts of the gospel." An infinitesimal flaw could be observed in his being "rather rigid in his requisitions . . . [and] confident in his own opinions." Otherwise he appears to have been without blemish.

Although music was his avocation he was fond of poetry and he admired some verses of Catharine's which appeared in *The Christian Spectator*. The admiration led to an introduction, a walk home from Litchfield Church after Lyman's sermon, an invitation to Sunday dinner, more walks home after services, more Sunday dinners, a quarrel and an engagement. Catharine seems to have had the sense to keep her incomparable suitor guessing for a brief period before "that betrothal took place . . . the realization of all my favorite dreams of earthly bliss. Affection, taste, ambition, everything most desirable to me and to family friends seemed secured."

The lovers played and sang at the piano, exchanged verses and indulged in all the engaging and innocent byplay of a seemly and happy courtship. Not even the New England Sabbath could dull their delight in each other. They planned their marriage for the spring of 1823, when Fisher should have returned from a year of study and travel in England and on the Continent. He sailed on the ship *Albion* on the first of April 1822. She was wrecked in May off the coast of Ireland and all but two of her twenty-three passengers were lost.

"After the first stunning effect was over," writes Catharine, "the next feeling was 'this is the indispensable sorrow! This is to save me from *eternal death*.' Shut up in entire seclusion, all my dearest hopes crushed, without hope or object in life, overwhelmed with grief, [I was] *horrified less at his dreadful death than at the awful apprehensions he himself had imparted that he was unprepared to die!*"

With Fisher's death the ancient and neglected deity had proclaimed himself like the Fenris wolf and slavered for the soul of the young scientist. His friends groaned for pity and terror. For this "model of every domestic, social and official virtue, so reverent to God, so tender as a son and brother, so conscientious and faithful as an instructor" was almost certainly damned, damned by his own showing as Catharine learned to her agony when his parents put their son's personal papers in her hands.

"Here I read his private records of *years* of almost superhuman effort to govern his mind and yet . . . all ended in failure; and this too without any murmuring or any accusation of anyone but himself. It was as he maintained, because he was so ungrateful, so hardened, so obstinately 'unwilling,' so averse from God and His service. . . . In not a single duty did he fail that the closest intimacy could discover; and yet . . . he had no love to God and was entirely 'unwilling' to love and serve Him."

There was no comfort, no hope, no help, not even the peace of annihilation. "At this period," says Catharine, "I almost lost my reason." Fisher's formidable virtues conspired to mock his bereaved lover. While Honesty put the question, Humility blew the coals and Mercy applied the hot irons. One frightful image succeeded another in Catharine's distraught imagination: Fisher writhing under a Promethean torment, wailing that he had ever been born, "the noble faculties of such a mind doomed to everlasting woe." He had made no public profession of conversion. His blameless behavior and irreproachable piety were meaningless. The only hope of his salvation lay in the faint possibility that he had experienced a saving grace in the hour of death when with bloodied face he stood brooding over one of the ship's compasses, crying the course of the *Albion,* aware apparently that nothing could save the vessel from foundering against the headlands of Kinsale.

Both at home and in public Catharine's friends hastened to treat her raw wounds with spiritual sulphuric acid. Her father could discern only the frailest hope that Fisher was saved and bade her turn her thoughts toward her own salvation. Dr. Emmons of Franklin said in his eulogy that there were grounds for hope (it was the best he could do) that Professor Fisher had suffered conversion at the end. In an encomium delivered at Yale, James Luce Kingsley added good measure, pressed down and running over, to Catharine's cup. Fisher was a nonpareil to be compared with Leibniz and Boscovich; further, "his uniform tenderness of conscience, the sacred regard which he always manifested for religion . . . raise in our minds a *presumption* of holy affections in the heart as the source from which this conduct flows. . . . We can hardly refrain from ascribing to Professor Fisher that personal piety which had he professed none who knew him would have doubted his sincerity. In indulging this pleasant hope we may indeed be deceived."

Many years later Harriet chose the ordeal of the Fisher family for the crux of her now all but forgotten novel, *The Minister's Wooing*. People who remembered Catharine's visit to Caleb and Sally Cushing Fisher after their son's death found that in this instance Harriet exaggerated nothing. But if Catharine suffered, she at least had within her the seeds of recovery. "The intelligent, tender, heartbroken mother," convinced of nothing save her son's sufferings in Hell, lay down and died. Into the mouth of the mother of her drowned hero Harriet puts her indictment of the mad god of her fathers and shouts him down.

> ". . . I cannot, will not, be resigned! — it is all hard, unjust, cruel! — to all eternity I will say so! To me there is no goodness, no justice, no mercy in anything! Life seems to me the most tremendous doom that can be inflicted on a helpless being! What had we done, that it should be sent upon us? Why were we made to love so, to hope so, — our hearts so full of feeling, and all the laws of Nature marching over

*us, never stopping for our agony? . . . think of those
awful ages of eternity! and then think of all God's
power and knowledge used on the lost to make them
suffer! think that all but the merest fragment of mankind have gone into this, — are in it now! The number of the elect is so small that we can scarce count
them for anything! Think what noble minds, what
warm, generous hearts, what splendid natures are
wrecked and thrown away by thousands and tens of
thousands! How we love each other! how our hearts
weave into each other! . . . And all this ends —
O God, how must it end? . . . it isn't my sorrow
only! What right have I to mourn? Is my son any
better than any mother's son? Thousands of thousands, whose mothers loved them as I love mine, have
gone there! . . .*

*"Dr. Hopkins says that this is all for the best, better
than it would have been in any other possible way, —
that God chose it because it was for a greater final
good, — that He not only chose it, but took means to
make it certain, — that He ordains every sin, and does
all that is necessary to make it certain, — that He
creates the vessels of wrath and fits them for destruc-
tion, and that He has infinite knowledge by which
He can do it without violating their free agency.
. . . What a use of infinite knowledge! What if men
should do so? What if a father should take means
to make it certain that his poor little child should be
an abandoned wretch, without violating his free
agency? So much the worse, I say! They say He
does all this so that He may show to all eternity, by
their example, the evil nature of sin and its consequences! This is all that the greater part of the human
race have been used for yet; and it is all right, because
an overplus of infinite happiness is yet to be wrought*

out by it! It is not right! No possible amount of
good to ever so many creatures can make it right to
deprave ever so few; — happiness and misery cannot
be measured so! . . . Yet they say our salvation de-
pends on our loving God, — loving Him better than
ourselves, — loving Him better than our dearest
friends. It is impossible! It is contrary to the laws
of my nature! I can never love God! I can never
praise Him! I am lost! lost! lost! And what is worse,
I cannot redeem my friends! Oh, I could suffer, for-
ever, how willingly! — if I could save him! *But oh,*
eternity, eternity! Frightful, unspeakable woe! . . ."

Operatic as this passage is, it illustrates correctly the state
of mind of the Fishers and Catharine during the ghastly
summer and autumn of 1822.

To many minds abstract philosophy is inimical and religion, save at its sweetest and simplest, incomprehensible
and therefore terrifying. Such people (and they make up
a large proportion of the human race) do not deal in symbol and paradox. The courts of theology, for all their
grandeur, are halls of homesickness and oppression to such
natures. Catharine's was one of these. She was active,
benevolent, warmhearted, civilized and sound, but it would
have taken a miracle of Cana to make her religious. Like
Fisher she was a victim of the remorseless New England
tradition which required that every man, woman and child,
however ungifted religiously, achieve the experience of a
religious genius. But while Catharine lived Fisher could
not be left in Hell. Thus, equipped with a piety that was
in her case little more than a Pavlovian reflex, induced by
stimuli quite beyond her reason or control, she prepared to

attack the validity of the blood-stained idol of the orthodox
and free Fisher from Death's dark prison. She was not
quite equal to the whirlwind doom of Francesca da Rimini:
she was vexed for her own soul as she quaked for Fisher's,
but since he languished in Calvinist chains, Catharine, dis-
guised as a philosopher, dared to descend to the catacombs
of Jonathan Edwards' edifice to release him.

"The first change of mind I now recall," she says, "was
an outburst of indignation and abhorrence. I remember
once rising as I was about to offer my usual, now hopeless
prayer, with a feeling very like this: that such a god did
not deserve to be loved; that I would not love him if I
could and I was glad I did not." In this mood she launched
her attack with the premise "There must be a dreadful mistake somewhere." Proceeding from this debatable ground
and using twenty words where two would do, Catharine
undertakes to show that God and the Christian religion are
not in violation of common sense. Herein lies the essence of
her argument and it is not easily or briefly resolved as *The
Letters on the Difficulties of Religion* attest at length.

"I can find no comfort in looking for the sad and terrific
probabilities of reason," she sighs, and fortunately does not
try too hard. Palpably God is incomprehensible. He per-
mits extraordinary things. Herod massacres the Innocents
and amiable gamblers ruin themselves and their families
in full view of Omnipotence; the good die young and
dealers in human misery wax old and prosperous. Reason
collapses under the weight of the puzzle. But in attempting
to meet its demands Catharine hit upon a few truths as
satisfyingly self-evident to her as anything in the Declara-

tion of Independence. She discovered them by answering a lot of questions that Edwards never propounded. God does not require of us what we are unable to perform, and Almighty Power is what is possible in the nature of things and compatible with the idea of universal benevolence. Predestined damnation is *not* compatible with universal benevolence and therefore not possible in the nature of things.

Then what decides the state of man after death? Character, she answers. Ah, but the Bible does not teach that any trait of character is a prerequisite to salvation. Then what are the causes of the love of God toward His creature? "Physical beauty!" cries plain Catharine, attributing to Heaven itself a love of Fisher's beauty. Physical power, moral principles in resisting temptation, intellectual superiority, the power of giving and appreciating affection, true love of God: these she shows are the essentials to salvation.

It was a fearful task and it was ill performed, since Catharine was no more fitted for such chop-logic disputing than is a tone-deaf person for musical composition. Half strangled in syntax, scorched by contradiction, pulled down in her tracks by metaphor and simile, she pushed through the labyrinth of her thesis to her conclusion and her satisfaction. Her inability to assimilate opposed truths and her ignorance of the metamorphoses of the mystic saved her where a stronger logician would have collapsed midway of the dissertation. She was happily able to demonstrate that the merciless system of Jonathan Edwards was of no use for practical purposes and the redeemed soul (Fisher's in this case) rises through the argument "by supernatural divine influence" to the realms of bliss where common sense and universal benevolence unite in assigning it.

She not only convinced herself; she convinced Lyman. His women had been too much for him. Heresy exploded in him like a nova and he defended it until his death. Three times he faced trial before an ecclesiastical court for his daring views on the Everlasting Mercy. When Catharine published the *Letters on the Difficulties of Religion* in 1836, the orthodox lowed like cattle in a slaughterhouse, and to no more purpose. History was against them and they were obviously predestined to defeat and oblivion. Free inquiry into the sciences, an aroused public conscience, basing its religion on the cry "By their fruits ye shall know them," a world changed out of all recognition by steam and by chemistry combined to hurry them from the world and bury them deep. Congregationalism, its fever burned out, exchanged the fear of God for an attitude of respectful admiration.

The romantic chapter of Catharine's life closed with the refutation of Edwards. Her heart lay under the sea with Fisher but it seems to have lain at peace. Even in the midst of her spiritual struggles she acknowledged the desirability of keeping body and soul (whether elect or not) together, and this impulse, coupled with a desire to "do good," led her into teaching. Fisher had left her two thousand dollars. With this capital, after a few weeks of cramming (Day's *Algebra* in five weeks) and a hard look at Latin, Hebrew, French and Emmanuel Kant, she opened the Hartford Female Seminary and became at twenty-two a popular and successful headmistress.

She lived for seventy-eight driving years, teaching, traveling, lecturing and writing on behalf of women's education and civilized legislation for children. She was not born a Connecticut Calvinist for nothing and she clung to her heresies, sometimes to her great personal cost, and also to her curls, and took them with a gathering eccentricity to her grave. To her last day she wore on her finger Alexander Metcalf Fisher's engagement ring, denying herself all other ornament. She grew dictatorial, vague and comically antique. When she joined the Porter family in Hartford for hymn singing she refused to join in the chorus which runs, "I am nothing, Lord, nothing — thou art all, all." "I am *not* nothing," said Catharine Beecher.

The courage that screamed down the terrible puppet of the Calvinists was not the less courage because the thing was after all merely a puppet. One of our tragic heroes held his strings. He was the failed creation of a great natural artist, a Punch and Judy monstrosity, hiding by its antics the nobility of the scene and by its noise the splendor of Jonathan Edwards' dialogue with Creation. For Edwards stands at the apex of Catharine's story (like all good love stories hers is a triangle), the dark giant who gave shape to the American conscience, suffering under the chastisement of an eternal misapprehension.

Edwards' theological certainties subside, useless and harmless as the properties of a stage villain. But something of his line of thought persisted to shape such men as Fisher and in a later generation Willard Gibbs. The foundations of the New England Hell crumbled when men turned their scrutiny to the structure of light-waves. The proportion of sin to eternity lost meaning under the impact of the exploration of the conservation of energy. The laboratory and not the pulpit would show what Edwards failed to teach his listeners, "how all arts and sciences, the more they are perfected the more they issue in divinity and coincide with it and appear to be parts of it."

THE PARSON AND THE BLUESTOCKING

WHEN WE SCAN the newspapers of New England for the year 1847 we are inclined to marvel at what failed to constitute a scandal in those pre-atomic times. Inserted among notices of mortgage sales and advertisements for elixirs guaranteed to cure everything from the croup to a dropped womb we come upon such stirring accounts as that of Eliza McCormick, a servant girl who masqueraded as a bank clerk on her Sundays off and attempted the seduction of other servant girls. "She is thought to be," remarked the journalist who covered the story, "the same person who figured at Galt a short time since under the disguise of a sick sailor."

Eliza figured no further in the public press that spring, although a number of eccentric cases succeeded her. Two fine baby boys in an expensive lying-in establishment were mixed up — so hopelessly that their distracted mothers were urged simply to pick a child and go home since there was no possible way of deciding which infant was whose. A man in Florida paid out a grudge by capturing the object of his illwill, tying him to an alligator and then setting fire to the alligator with the unhappiest consequences for both man and beast. Princess Demdoff, dressed in a man's clothes, horsewhipped her husband's mistress. A member of a highly respected New England family joined an Arab tribe and became notable for his war chant, "Old Hundred," which he rendered with an invincible Yankee twang as he galloped with his Bedouins into battle.

Not one of these items, newsworthy as they may now strike us, merited more than two inches of space in any Connecticut paper. The scandal of the year was the affair of Miss Delia Bacon and the Reverend Alexander MacWhorter.

At the time of this tribulation Delia Bacon had not yet become famous as one of the chief supporters of the theory that William Shakespeare was merely a pseudonym for Sir Francis Bacon, Sir Walter Raleigh and others. A highbred bluestocking of thirty-five, she met Alexander MacWhorter, a twenty-three-year-old clergyman in the New Haven boardinghouse where they were both living; and in spite of the unfavorable disparity in their ages they fell in love, or so Miss Bacon ultimately asserted. MacWhorter for his part swore to the contrary. The consequences of their encounter turned out to be something that was bigger than both of them. Their lovers' quarrel was absorbed into a wrangle for authority, intemperate and unseemly, between the parochial clergy of the city of New Haven and the faculty of the Yale Divinity School. The Congregational Church was touched on the raw, for MacWhorter was the protégé of Nathaniel William Taylor, professor of didactic theology at Yale and one of the most powerful men in Connecticut. Delia, on the other hand, was not only a celebrated *femme savante* but the sister of Taylor's close friend Leonard Bacon, pastor of the First Church of Christ (or Center Church), the fountainhead of Connecticut Calvinism and chief shrine of the Establishment in the Commonwealth.

New Haven in the forties was a gay city and at that time one of the handsomest towns in New England. In defiance perhaps of its Cromwellian beginnings (it had been a refuge for regicides during the Restoration) and the monastic pattern of its university, it was proud of its newly formed Beethoven society, its good taverns and the beauty and wit of its women. Its chief commodity, however, was the Congregational clergy. Ministers served as the backbone of its society, its principal export and finest ornament.

In addition to its ghostly powers the priest caste of New Haven exercised considerable temporal ones, inasmuch as the clergy owned a large proportion of the land of the Commonwealth. Churchmen were thus able to perform with scarifying audacity the roles of both yogi and commissar, governing a demesne whose limits stretched from the cradle to well beyond the grave. Of this the elders whose duty it was to license young divines were keenly aware. The Church required that the characters of her ministers be unimpeachable. His scholarship, his morals and his orthodoxy underwent the severest scrutiny before the Congregational hobbledehoy ascended the pulpit. Although here and there a misfit appeared — such as the Reverend Azel Backus, who "could not keep his drolleries out of the pulpit" and "lived a life of questionable propriety" while the souls under his care tittered their way to perdition — he seems to have been as odd as an owl trooping among chickens. Clergymen in general avoided levity, lived by the book, mastered the Greek, Latin and Hebrew tongues, married blameless behavior to a set of stern beliefs and graced it all with the uses and accomplishments of a gentleman. Such a man was Nathaniel Taylor, the Rhadamanthus of Delia Bacon's ordeal, and such a man was his antagonist, Leonard Bacon.

A hundred years earlier New Haven had had no God but Yahweh, and Jonathan Edwards was his prophet. The brimstone perorations that sizzled from New England pulpits had caused women to faint and strong men to shudder in their beds at the mere recollection. But by 1845 a younger and more impressionable generation was bringing a Byronic sensibility to the exacerbated conscience of Calvinism. (Byron seems to have had great charm for the adherents of this savage creed: there was an unmistakable allure in one so militantly, not to say joyously, damned).

The old Calvinists were poulticing the bruises received from the Unitarians and the heretical Henry Ward Beecher; and though Nathaniel Taylor preached on infant damnation, one senses that he was not wholly for it. He had even made a strong case for free will in his controversy with Bennet Tyler twenty years previously. But now from "bawling and quarreling over the Trinity" the parsons and their parishioners had fallen victim to a fit of salvation by works. The salvation-through-grace-alone faction smoldered in the ascendancy only within the university, free will notwithstanding. The rank-and-file parish priest boomed with reforming zeal, replacing the totemic deity with something that closely resembled a kindly social worker. Antislavery was a hotter issue than antimonianism. Yahweh suffered further from a rising cluster of scientists who ignored him and from women — intellectual women, such women as Lyman Beecher's wives and daughters — who simply regarded him as a frightful mistake.

The doctrinaire Calvinists had heard themselves roundly refuted by Delia Bacon's mentor, Catharine Beecher, in 1836. Delia's assault on MacWhorter took on the character of a thumping blow delivered at the infallibility of the Establishment, and his misuse of her confirmed the opposition in its suspicion that predestination made poor preaching and worse practice. New Haven split over the matter like a melon in the sun.

In a city less remorselessly dynastic so ragged a rent in the garment of civic unity might not have shown so threadbare. But here where Days married Shermans and Blakes married Thachers and Bacons married Woolseys and the issue married back into the kith while Taylors stood godparents to first-born Bacon babies, it was clear that death could not sunder the family party, but, shockingly, Delia Bacon could.

The Bacon family was of the church churchly and what it lacked in earthly goods it more than made up for in spiritual dignities and prestige. Leonard and Delia were the children of a missionary, David Bacon, and both had been born in the vicinity of that outpost of the Connecticut empire now known as Detroit. After Delia Salter was born in 1811, David gave up his attempt to establish Heaven on earth at Tallmadge, Ohio, and died heartbroken and debt-ridden, leaving his widow Alice with six children to rear. By various shifts she managed to educate all six. Leonard was graduated from Yale at eighteen, finished his theological studies at Andover and entered on his pastorate at Center Church at twenty-three years of age. Delia, the youngest and most promising of the girls, early began to raise both hopes and apprehensions in the bosoms of her relatives. Clever, mercurial and ambitious, she did not seem to know the meaning of the word moderation. When she caught the mumps, her sister Alice wrote to Leonard in real consternation that "Delia has a swelled face and has lost her reason." Delia's faculty for mislaying this article continued to be a source of genuine anxiety, but when in possession of her wits she showed herself industrious as a spider and ready to attack almost any difficulty if she glimpsed the possibility of a reward. "Delia will do almost anything for money," wrote the hard-pressed Mrs. Bacon in a letter to her son Leonard containing a doleful account of the family's financial anxieties.

The little girl's natural liveliness was tempered with spasms of religious melancholy, in those days common among children as measles or chicken pox. "Your sister has resisted the Holy Spirit and He has departed from me," she wrote at the age of ten to Leonard. "When I think of it I tremble . . . Oh what will become of me when I leave this vain, transitory world and rise before my God in judgment? Cease not to pray for me for I have neglected the offers of salvation. I have despised my dear Redeemer but there is still mercy in Him who is able to save."

When Delia was about eleven some friends of her mother's took her under their charge and enrolled her as a pupil in the Female Seminary at Hartford, recently established by the uproarious Lyman Beecher's eldest daughter, Catharine. Here the volatile, bright-eyed youngster became a favorite not only with her teachers but with a fellow pupil, Catharine's droll, exquisite and spirited little sister, Harriet. Here is the child Delia as her twenty-two-year-old headmistress saw her: "An agreeable person, a pleasing and intelligent countenance, and eye of deep and earnest espression, a melodious voice, a fervid imagination and the embryo of rare gifts of eloquence."

Miss Beecher's affection for the child did not blind her to Delia's flaws. The little girl's longing for excellence was based as much on a desire for applause as a devotion to perfection. Love, recognition and literary notoriety were far too dear to her in Catharine's estimation. Delia aimed for prizes and, when these eluded her, her disappointment was out of all proportion to the value that should have been placed on such trifles. Catharine describes her as a brilliant improvisor but deficient when it came to organizing her material and getting it down according to the rules of unity, coherence and emphasis. Worse, she was only intermittently pious, performing her religious duties sketchily enough to cause some concern as to the state of her soul. Catharine candidly admits that Delia was a handful. Fiercely competitive, she could not endure to see the work of others valued above her own, and when, as frequently happened, some other student gained the first place in class her sufferings from jealousy were extreme. Her schoolfellows, who seem to have been a good-natured lot, were frequently reduced to forgetting their own triumphs in an effort to comfort and encourage her.

"Her keen sensibility," continues Catharine, "her transparency, sincerity and impulsiveness, the dangerous power of keen and witty expression . . . would make her an object of unjust depreciation. The persons . . . who were the objects of her regard would almost immediately become enthusiastic admirers while those who in any way came into antagonism would be as decided in their dislike."

Only one likeness of Delia exists, a daguerreotype taken when she was in her forties. By all accounts it does not do her justice. The rich eye, the fine mobility of feature, the translucent complexion, which though pale seemed to glow, are all absent. The woman whom Hawthorne described as "majestic . . . graceful," full of vivacity, dignity and charm has nothing in common with the strained and cynically smiling personage of the picture. It is a portrait of a sardonically tilted head, a warped mouth, two veined hands, a bonnet and a cashmere shawl. Little is revealed of the creature who caught the attention of Emerson, Carlyle and Hawthorne, the accomplished *salonnière* whose allure was described by a large group of witnesses as almost mesmeric.

"A beautiful being," declared Elizabeth Peabody in a letter to Leonard Bacon after Delia's death. "A glorious and wonderful work of nature, most unhappily environed by uncongenial circumstances in many respects. Her entire unworldliness, her childlike character inspired me with a tenderness without bounds." But Miss Peabody strikes a dissonance in her paean. Unbounded tenderness did not prevent Hawthorne's shrewd sister-in-law from knowing that Delia "suffered . . . from the fear that I would steal her secret [the Shakespearean cipher] and publish it myself."

In her twenties and early thirties Delia's character partook apparently of the Victorian image of a perfect lady. She was a virtuous daughter and sister, religious and nice to the point of prudishness in her relations with the opposite sex. Had it not been for her almost excessive refinement she might have earned a reputation for "strong-mindedness" through her evident indifference to male admiration. Throughout her youth she gave no signs of having any interest in men at all save those included in her immediate family. At fifteen she had decided to become a teacher, but she soon discovered that classroom instruction did not promise the kind of reward that she wanted. She attempted a school of her own, as Miss Beecher had done so successfully, but the venture failed and she wavered to writing. She had an errant fancy, could tell a tale with spirit, define a character and summon up a landscape with poetic immediacy. She tackled historical romance and did not scruple to write drama in verse. *Tales of the Puritans* and *The Bride of Fort Edward* were published and brought her neither fame nor fortune, but they led ultimately to the lecture platform. Delia had a remarkable propensity for oratory and was, like her brother, capable of haranguing an audience for hours together without tiring either it or herself.

The wives and daughters of her brother's colleagues were in transports about her. She lectured on classical antiquity, the Renaissance and on English letters in both

Boston and New Haven; her select audience of well-born, well-endowed ladies paid highly for the privilege of hearing her. As she stood before two statues of Diana and Apollo (tributes from admiring listeners), fragile and fiery, dressed always in black, which set off her delicate style of beauty to perfection, she struck the spectators as a Tennysonian princess, an enchanting priestess at the shrine of the Muses.

While Delia was in the way of accumulating if not a fortune a pretty good living and the literary fame that she had so passionately longed for as a schoolgirl, she was not the only woman in New Haven who combined personal magnetism with intellectual eminence. At 77 Elm Street a young rival was putting the polish on a series of lustrous attainments. Henrietta Whitney Blake was at this time in her early twenties, a tall dark girl, formidably accomplished. She was a good classical scholar and is reliably reported to have thrown over an eligible *parti* for sending her a Greek ode disfigured by false quantities.

Unlike Delia Bacon, Henrietta was born rich, one of the ten children of Eli Whitney Blake, inventor of the Blake stone-crusher. Eli Whitney's cotton gin also loomed in her background. According to one of her admirers, James Hadley, she "avowed and gloried in a delightful perversity of taste."

The Blakes shared with the Bacons, the Taylors, the Woolseys, the Baldwins and a few other privileged families a comfortable eminence in the exclusive New Haven hierarchy, and it was toward this company that the Reverend Alexander MacWhorter, the only son of a doting widow from New Jersey, directed his innocent footsteps. Possessing a good income, a good profile and an engaging address, the gentle youth made a charming impression. Nathaniel Taylor took him under his special protection and Leonard Bacon's signature was one of those adorning the articles licensing him to preach. He had won a reputation as a scholar during his undergraduate days at Yale and was considered to have a pretty, if slightly condescending, wit. Beyond these attractions he seems to have shared with Delia Bacon an indefinable allure. People flocked about him, especially men, although women liked him too. He laid claim to an excessive naïveté where women were concerned but he took pains that no false quantities should mar his interchange with Henrietta Blake.

On becoming a licentiate in the Congregational Church he moved into the boardinghouse where Delia Bacon lived, fixed his large eyes on her and breathed a longing to know her. The recipient of this confidence was a classmate, Robert W. Forbes, for whom Delia had conceived one of her celebrated dislikes. She considered him flimsy and quite unfit to attend the levees that she was in the habit of holding in her rooms for the benefit of her students and their parents. She had, however, nothing against MacWhorter, and with the arrogance of a de Staël and without waiting for a formal introduction she sent him a note indicating her willingness to receive him but pointedly excluding Forbes.

Delia's initial objections to Forbes remain mantled in mystery. Catharine Beecher, Delia's staunchest defender, admits that she cannot account for them. But it was enough that Miss Bacon did not like him and would not have him on her premises, although she had known him since his childhood and had even been a guest of his family. The slight cankered him vilely. The flirtatious licentiate, however, applied a certain balm by reading the note of invitation aloud to his neglected friend and making good fun of a maiden lady, old enough to know better, unabashedly scurrying after a rich young man. MacWhorter also wrote a most entertaining letter to his friend the Reverend Alexander Huntingdon Clapp, parson of the Congregational Church at Brattleboro, Vermont, describing the whole amusing episode and, without precisely saying so, hinting that Miss Bacon's behavior had been unbecomingly forward.

He concealed this state of things from Delia, however, and having gained admission to her rooms, rather rapidly cemented the friendship, which under this treatment shortly flowered into a love which was "pure," "fervent," but to Delia's annoyance and her family's incredulous scorn, "fraternal."

Victorian courtships were things of sighs and glances, of half-uttered exclamations, blushes and pallors, pleasing confusions, and devoted and particular attentions, signs as cloudy as the symptoms of typhoid fever but as decided and contagious as the disease itself. This one was no exception and was moreover carried on at one time in the full glare of Harriet Beecher Stowe, whose evidence makes it clear that MacWhorter pressed his suit as zestfully as any pouter pigeon. "The most open, direct, above-ground, positive and explicit piece of wooing that was ever performed under my own particular observation . . . such as nothing but a positive engagement would justify any gentleman and Christian in pursuing."

To do her justice, it appears that Delia had doubts as to the wisdom and propriety of this courtship. She found MacWhorter's attentions disconcerting. When she appeared at the boardinghouse breakfast table he would leave his seat to join her and pledge her in his second cup of coffee. His eyes followed her wherever she went. Other ladies in the house rallied her on her conquest. Like Mrs. Stowe they had never seen such unmistakable signs of devotion. Clearly, MacWhorter was incapable of giving his thoughts to anybody but Miss Bacon. Children noticed it, servants noticed it and with some distaste the Bacon family was forced to notice it. Delia was flustered. She feared that MacWhorter, taking advantage of the difference in their ages, had "chosen to insult her with unmeaning expressions of his regard."

Common sense had a premature triumph and Delia shifted her quarters to her brother's house, where MacWhorter took the earliest opportunity of calling and was as assiduous as ever. Delia's little nephews were employed as messengers between the lovers. Delia's mother expressed dissatisfaction with the turn of events. She asked her daughter what she had in mind. The answer was not very reassuring. "She assured me again and again that nothing would induce her to marry him and that she much desired and must have the opportunity of telling him so."

Delia had, in short, maneuvered herself into the position of being forced to sue for a proposal of marriage in order to refuse it. In her mother's presence she wrote to MacWhorter, who had gone to Saratoga, and sent the letter off. He replied at once and the harassed Delia dutifully handed the letter to Mrs. Bacon.

"It contained a declaration of warm, eternal, undying affection," declared Mrs. Bacon. "I distinctly remember the expression: 'I have loved you purely, fervently.' He assured her . . . that his love for her was a love which no change of circumstance could alter and that even though she should hate him it would make no difference: that he should love her in life and in death and beyond it." But there was a further disquieting allusion to loving her "as a brother." Mrs. Bacon had never heard of such a thing as fraternal love between grownups, believed it to be an impossibility of nature and repugnant besides. Delia was reduced to telling MacWhorter that she could not be a sister to him and he countered with the question was "not another relationship possible?" What other he did not say.

With her mother's views so painfully clear and mindful that her brother was diverted from antislavery legislation, the colonization of Africa, the annexation of Nebraska, the conversion of China, Center Church, his eleven children and his new second wife to a thoroughly disapproving view of his sister's case, Delia decided to try a change of air. She set out for Brattleboro, Vermont, and MacWhorter came tumbling after. He even canceled an engagement to pinch-hit in a fellow preacher's pulpit in order to accompany her on the last lap of her journey to the spa.

For ten weeks Delia and MacWhorter remained at Brattleboro. During that time he danced constant attendance. His thoughts, his looks, the very slant of his shoulders were all directed toward her. They walked together, talked almost exclusively to each other — in fact so absorbed were they in their liaison that the other guests in the hotel where they had lodgings made themselves scarce when Delia and MacWhorter took possession of the parlor rather than intrude upon them. To all of this the people who ran the inn testified exuberantly.

One person who was not convinced was MacWhorter's friend Alexander Clapp, the minister of Brattleboro. He and his giddy young wife refuted the whole notion of a love affair between the elderly Miss Bacon and the young minister as absurd. Mrs. Stowe, however, who had arrived in Vermont with her husband, was satisfied that what she saw must lead to marriage. She reported her findings to her sister Catharine, and shortly after doing so she encountered Robert Forbes. Rumors of the engagement had reached him and he was seething like a kid in its mother's milk. His friend MacWhorter was a helpless pawn in a series of nefarious moves by Miss Bacon. She had been the pursuer from the beginning. She was a woman who lived by her talents, MacWhorter was a man of property; she was of an unsuitable age; she must be a schemer. She had lain in wait for MacWhorter at another's house where he had not thought to find her and had written to him without benefit of a previous introduction. Her immodest behavior justified MacWhorter in amusing himself to his heart's content at her expense.

Mrs. Stowe was bewildered and distressed. "It displeased me to hear that you had written a note prior to the introduction," she wrote Delia later.

It seems little enough now — a display of reciprocal interest on the part of a lady and a gentleman in the well-chaperoned atmosphere of a family hotel, a few letters containing lofty sentiments couched in the ornate language of the era. The whole ritual seems so stylized that it carries about as much conviction as the antics of the figures in a willow-ware plate. But to the people of the year 1846 the parson and the bluestocking were chief actors in a drama as compelling as a bullfight, and New Haven society wanted its moment of truth.

It did not come. Miss Beecher arrived in the Green Mountains and asked Delia point-blank what her matrimonial prospects were. When questioned Delia proved as unmanageable at thirty-five as she had been at eleven.

"What shall I say if people ask me if you are to marry him?" inquired Miss Beecher.

"Say what you please," was the reply.

"Shall it be called a platonic flirtation?" pursued Miss Beecher.

"Say whatever you think best," evaded Delia. She had been jilted and she knew it. MacWhorter had returned to New Haven and Leonard Bacon had tackled him with an excited request for an explanation of the attentions paid to Delia.

"What attentions?" asked MacWhorter. He vehemently denied that he had courted Delia Bacon. He would not have his friends think him such a fool, he told Forbes. There had been no sentiment on his side, "not a thimbleful." He had lent himself to the affair only to help Delia save face. She had shown a preference for him. She had actually proposed to him. In the circumstances he had behaved exactly as he ought.

Alexander MacWhorter defies interpretation. There is

really no explaining him. If Delia had proposed to him on one occasion why did he not thank her for the offer and be off? And if, as he now told Roger Baldwin, the former governor of Connecticut, she proposed not once but five separate times, he must have been insatiable for punishment to have remained in Brattleboro for ten weeks, conspicuously devoting himself to her while enjoying the use of a pair of legs. Baldwin, who had submitted to MacWhorter's disclosures with reluctance, thought the fellow a rare fool and said as much.

The gossip in New Haven had by now, thanks to the misprized Robert Forbes and the Clapps, reached scurrilous proportions. Delia was totally compromised. Either she had been caught in a serious breach of decorum or she was the victim of a shameless intrigue at the hands of that "clerical Lothario," as MacWhorter was subsequently labeled in the public press. The Bacon family began to buckle on the armor of righteousness and Leonard Bacon raised his hatchet-head like a tomahawk for the scalp of the licentiate. The young man was guilty of slander, libel and conduct unbecoming a clergyman and a gentleman and should therefore be declared unfit to preach the gospel.

It was not to be supposed that MacWhorter and his friends would accede to this solution to Delia's vexations. He announced that he could produce evidence that Delia had been the active party throughout the whole affair and that if the Bacon family did not refrain from its persecutions he would be forced to defend himself by making Delia's correspondence public. Robert Forbes and his cousin, Jane Fitch, claimed to have seen it already. In that

case, argued Leonard Bacon, an investigation was impera-
tive. Either a man was fit to be a minister or he was not,
and if MacWhorter was innocent of the conduct imputed
to him by Delia and her friends he must prove it.

No, said MacWhorter and his partisans. The licentiate
would prove nothing. Let the Bacons prove their case.

Delia at first had hoped to close the chapter in the classic
manner with the burning of letters and the remission of
gifts. When she failed to receive her letters and learned
that they had fallen into the hands of Forbes, Clapp and
such girls as the satirical Henrietta Blake and malicious little
Jane Fitch, she rose to a falcon's fury that momentarily
shook even MacWhorter's leaden poise. Her ultimatum to
him announced that she had seen the whites of his eyes and
was prepared to shoot.

> *You certainly cannot but be aware that the repre-
> sentations which are generally made here with regard
> to my relations to you are wholly and basely untrue.
> ... You know that my regard for you was one which
> such a devotion as yours could hardly fail to inspire
> in a heart not wholly insensible to kindness. Need
> I remind you of that devotion? ... The whole vocabu-
> lary of poetic feeling has been exhausted to convey it
> to me; not in writing, indeed, for you have been quite
> careful not to commit yourself in this way. . . . You
> have read my letters to your friends. Did you read
> them* all? *Were there no suppressed passages? Did you
> tell them of the circumstances that originated them?
> Did you tell them of those expressions of impassioned
> sentiment without which they would not have been
> written? Did you tell them that I had distinctly* de-
> clined *the honor to which I am represented as having*

*aspired? . . . Representations, the most humiliating
to me, the most degrading that were ever fastened on
a woman of reputation, are referred to you as their
author. You have made it necessary for me to make
statements on this subject in my own defense. . . .
I had once some influence here and weakened and
wasted as it is, such as it is I will use it to the utmost.
You may read this letter to as many of your acquaintance as you please. I do not wish for any answer. . . .
All I ask of you is to* send me my letters.

The beleaguered MacWhorter received this letter at the
house of Nathaniel Taylor, where he was staying. When
his reply to it was returned to him unopened, he glimpsed
an alarming threat to his career. The Bacons were implacable, and if Nathaniel Taylor should take their part impeachment was virtually certain. In desperation he threw
himself on the mercy of Mrs. Taylor and her daughter,
Mrs. Noah Porter. He must have had stupendous powers
of persuasion. In spite of their long friendship with the
Bacons, which included Delia, and notwithstanding their
undisguised disapproval of MacWhorter's protracted sojourn in Brattleboro, his protestations of innocence won
them over. They promised to warn him of any impending
crisis, by crisis meaning the moment when the business
should come to the attention of the professor of didactic
theology.

The crisis came that afternoon in the interval between
tea and dinner and gallantly MacWhorter met it, shielded
by the crinolines of the Taylor ladies. Dr. Taylor heard
MacWhorter out sympathetically. Having endorsed the
young man in the community he chose not to take sides

but rather to make peace between the parties and hush things up. With this purpose Taylor called on Delia, bearing with him MacWhorter's peace terms. Quite simply they were as follows: if Delia would abstain from defending her "delicacy" and withdraw her accusations, Mac-Whorter would suppress his "evidence" against her. If not he would be forced to vindicate his honor by bringing a charge of slander against her. The Bacon family as one man indignantly rejected such a course. Taylor's olive branch might as well have been gunpowder thrown on the conflagration. The Bacons would not hold their tongues, would not bargain and would have the case tried.

The hearing was convened in Jeremiah Day's house (he had just resigned the presidency of Yale in the hope of spending his last days in peace and quiet). Twenty-three exasperated divines met together to try one of their own in a case of ill-considered coquetry. The parish clergy, headed by Bacon, lined up for Delia. The university theologians rallied around Taylor and MacWhorter.

Ponderously the inquiry lumbered on its way while the Day parlor shivered under oratory bedizened with classical allusions and ominous references to the Old Testament. Henrietta Blake from the perspective of Cornwall Bridge, whither she had discreetly decamped following the receipt of a severe letter from Dr. Bacon rating her for having let her eyes fall on Delia Bacon's letters, fairly glistened with moral indignation as the mail brought her almost daily accounts of the trial.

"*Poor* Mr. MacWhorter!" Among other things Miss Bacon had remarked that "Hettie Blake is doing her

LEONARD BACON

From a silhouette, dated 1841, in the possession of the author

"his hatchet-head like a tomahawk" (*page 111*)

DELIA BACON

From the author's collection

"Ophelia, wearing her rue with a difference"
(*page 118*)

prettiest to obtain Mr. MacWhorter," she wrote to her sister Mary. Then came, one supposes, a Dickensian toss of curls, an enchanting *moue*. "Now I think it very likely that I was doing my prettiest to Mr. MacWhorter. I'm sure I hope I always do to everybody and if I wasn't doing it to him I was making him an exception which I don't suppose I did."

Sarah Thacher, Hettie's cousin, added a postscript: "All that I have to say is!!!?? . . . What *is* Miss Bacon made of? If I were a medical student I should wait anxiously for her demise in order to procure a post mortem analysation. As to Mr. MacWhorter, his evidence seems to come out strong enough but I am not prepared to swallow *whole* all *his* simple negations. What a disgusting concern it is. . . . Do you seriously believe that anybody tells the truth nowadays?"

The committee ruled that in view of Leonard Bacon's demand for impeachment the burden of proof lay with him. His faction resorted to comparing Taylor to John King, the London blackmailer of women, while the defense retaliated by hinting that Delia had tampered with the correspondence made available to the court. Further, a witness, John Lord, was heard from who testified to the happiness of also having received proposals of marriage from Delia. Benjamin Silliman, the elder, who had been made privy to her correspondence at an early date, saved her from the imputation of forgery. In the matter of the second charge Delia was able to prove that the surprise witness had proposed to her some years earlier and been rejected.

Delia trembled and wept when giving her testimony;

MacWhorter maintained an ineffable calm. He did not attempt to deny what could not be denied. He merely stuck to his original story. He was not responsible for Delia's misconstruction of his intentions. His behavior was perfectly consonant with that appropriate to a minister of the gospel. The issue was clear enough. Justinian himself could not have tried either Delia or MacWhorter for going to a Vermont spa, although both were guilty of doing so.

The decision when it came showed frenzied footwork. Eleven of the members found for Delia, twelve for Mac-Whorter. On the one hand it was agreed that the licentiate had been "in a greater or less degree imprudent in his conduct." "But," added the clergymen, "by which we do not intend to imply that what the aforesaid licentiate has reported of the relative of the complainant is true." They further advised that a committee of three should be appointed "to give with Christian and paternal kindness such admonition to him as in their view the case may require."

MacWhorter's Pyrrhic victory was a rout for Delia. Nothing short of his impeachment could have saved her mangled fame. The less respectable portions of the press were making revelry over her sufferings at the hands of her lover, her friends were censorious or, like Catharine Beecher, ruinously overzealous in her defense, and her brother was talking grimly of retiring from the pulpit and taking up teaching in some retired spot.

"God does not need my labor," she cried. "He appoints me to suffer."

In her outrage and frustration she turned to the attack on William Shakespeare, a subject she had discussed with

MacWhorter in happier days. Her journey to England, made with the purpose of proving her thesis, ended in the church at Stratford-on-Avon, where the sexton found her, mad as the baker's daughter, shuddering at the sight of Shakespeare's unopened tomb. She was briefly confined in the asylum in the Forest of Arden until her family, with whom she had quarreled bitterly, brought her back to Connecticut. She died in the Hartford Retreat at the age of forty-six, lucid and reconciled to her friends, and asking for a last look at the picture of her father, who had grieved himself to death because he could not bring the Kingdom of God to the wilderness in his generation.

Alexander MacWhorter continued to preach the gospel and to bother his friends with his theory of the infinite divisibility of magnitude and to puzzle them with the Baconian heresy to which he remained (perhaps sentimentally) attached. In 1852 Henrietta gave rein to her delightful perversity of taste and married him, to her father's unconcealed dismay. After holding a teaching post in New York State for a year, MacWhorter returned to New Haven with Henrietta for a visit to Eli Blake and further infuriated the old gentleman by staying for twenty years. Mr. Blake, as one of his granddaughters put it, "was too honest to pretend a cordiality he did not feel." He was never known during those twenty years to have addressed his son-in-law directly. MacWhorter's own faction had come to regret the committee's decision. Vindicated, he lived to cause the Divinity School perpetual embarrassment because of his pusillanimous mode of life and the crashing dullness of his occasional sermons.

Leonard Bacon wholeheartedly forgave Nathaniel Taylor, and Eli Blake reaped the reward of his grand silence when MacWhorter concluded his visit to 77 Elm Street with his mortal span in 1880. Henrietta was inconsolable. She dutifully kept house for her father, however, until his death. With that event, which was long in coming, she shook the dust of New Haven from her sandal and ended her days merrily in a *pensione* in Siena, dying in 1901.

The investigation which had blacked the newspapers and wagged the tongues in 1847 was so far forgotten that people growing up ten years after had never heard of it. Delia alone of its chief performers is memorable. Her love affair was a badly managed farce, her life work, *The Philosophy of the Plays of Shakespere Unfolded,* is a marvelously contrived gargoyle, a monument to misapplied scholarship; and yet she emerges with dignity, a pathetic, even an engaging spectacle, like Ophelia, wearing her rue with a difference.

GOD AND WOMAN AT YALE

S IR," wrote Cotton Mather to Elihu Yale in 1698, "though you have your felicities in your family which I pray God continue and multiply, yet certainly if what is forming at New Haven might wear the name of Yale College it would be better than a name of sons and daughters. And your munificence might easily obtain for you such a commemoration and perpetuation of your valuable name as would be better than an Egyptian pyramid."

Elihu Yale, "a gentleman who greatly abounded in good humor and generosity," never raised up a legitimate son to God. He rejoiced in several daughters, but his only son by his lawful wedded wife died as an infant in Madras when Yale was agent for the East India Company and governor of Fort St. George. He had another son, Charles, by a woman named Mrs. Pavia, a Portuguese Jewess who lived openly and scandalously with Yale in his garden house in Madras. When her lover returned to England, Mrs. Pavia, who had prudently put something by, emigrated with Charles to Cape Town in South Africa. She devoted her leisure in the Dutch trading post to the design and construction of the tomb under which she and Yale's illegitimate son are both buried in the long shadow of Table Mountain.

Yale, along with being good-humored and generous, was sensual, greedy and arrogant, with an ungovernable temper. It is said that he once had an Indian groom hanged for riding out to the country without leave on a favorite horse. He was a sound administrator and money loved him and attached itself to him almost to the point of making a nuisance of itself. Glutted with his wealth and all but crushed under the weight of his possessions, Yale held one of the first public auctions in England in order to rid himself of his surplus goods, the spoils of his travels in the East, which were crowding him out of his house. And in a fit of his celebrated good humor, brought on by Cotton Mather's unctuous letter, he gave some of his surplus money to the college that was better than a pyramid and was instantly named for him. Greater names than his added their gifts. Sir Isaac Newton, Sir Richard Steele and Dean Berkeley of Down made donations. Berkeley acted in the belief that the institution would ultimately become an Anglican college — people in search of funds to endow academies with will lead anybody to believe anything — and the dean gave a library. In 1733 he also gave the rents from his farm, "Cloyne," in Newport for a scholarship known as the Dean's Bounty. The source of the bounty was Esther Vanhomrigh, Jonathan Swift's Vanessa, of whose will Berkeley was executor. But Yale gave the lion's share of the money, purchasing for himself immortality in

America and a somewhat niggardly and derivative epitaph in his own parish church in Wrexham:

> *Born in America, in Europe bred,*
> *In Afric travell'd, and in Asia wed,*
> *Where long he liv'd and thriv'd; at London dead.*
> *Much good, some Ill he did: so hope all's even,*
> *And that his soul thro' Mercy's gone to Heav'n.*
> > *You that survive and read, take care*
> > *For this most certain Exit to prepare,*
> > *For only the Actions of the Just,*
> > *Smell sweet and blossom in the dust.*

Yale was indisputably founded by men. They were orthodox Congregationalist clergymen, stout of heart and clear of purpose. They raised two hundred and forty pounds among themselves before they began applying for gifts, but they could not agree upon a spot in which to found the "Collegiate School" they had in mind. Some argued for Saybrook, some for Wethersfield, others for Hartford, "much being written and said — and with great bitterness" in favor of all three. They finally settled on New Haven, which contented nobody.

When New Haven first at Heaven's command arose from out of Long Island Sound she was at the time the order was given a mere fraction of a chain of volcanoes. Long-striding chicken-footed dinosaurs squelched about in the ooze and the area was subject to periodic explosions, a condition that has subsisted ever since in one form or another, although the volcano, rudely sheered off by an errant glacier, has lapsed into silence. The crenelated walls of East Rock and West Rock bear witness to Triassic splendors long gone to dust. The sea shimmers at the city's western shore. The sky above it is haunted by a ghost frigate which appears from time to time to warn of impending disaster. At sunrise when the mists begin to rise over the red wall of East Rock the White Lady of the Mist takes shape in the cloud and lures young men to pursue her up the face of the cliff, thus breaching a city ordinance and a university regulation. Neither jail nor fines nor suspension from their colleges deters them in the quest for the oread. From its beginnings monastic Yale, "the man-child . . . whereat we all rejoyce," as the college was described by its founders, has been badgered, bedeviled and beset by females. No institution ever put up a fiercer resistance — no woman's college exists at Yale to this day — but the struggle seems merely to prove that out-at-the-door is in-at-the-window. No sooner is one woman disposed of than another flutters up in her place. Yale might have done well to establish herself in the mountains rather than by the sea. Shore towns lie in the neighborhood of Aphrodite and her shrines sing beneath the waves. Every woman fancies herself a votary. New Haven girls gazed into their looking glasses and thanked God they were not as other women. The beauty of New Haven women became an accepted fact among themselves anyway. Massachusetts girls looked like codfish and New York was Dutch. When New Haven stood under fire from British gunboats during the Rebellion, Anna Jordan, fifteen years old and already a famous beauty, was sent by her fellow citizens to the Commander of the attacking vessels to deflect his attention from the town by plying him with drink and the sight of her regular features and symmetrical form. The device worked. New

Haven remained intact, and so, curiously, did Anna's virtue. The tale of her triumph over the British Navy somehow worked itself into her funeral sermon, preached by Leonard Bacon, the pastor of Center Church, three quarters of a century later. Her virtues were copious but the parson dwelt long and lovingly on her good looks almost as though they were an instance of God's favor and a sign of election. A reputation for beauty once firmly established is not to be shaken by its mere loss. New Haven women were beautiful — into their nineties if necessary — and nobody was allowed to ignore it, least of all New Haven men. When Benjamin Bacon became an usher at Groton in 1844 he so far forgot what was due to himself as to praise a Massachusetts girl. "You have been away from us girls for so long," wrote his sister Rebecca, "that you have forgotten how attractive we are. There is probably such a dearth of beauty in the polar regions where you are that a tolerable looking person seemed twice as wonderful by contrast."

In the eighteenth century the ladies had not yet begun to fight. They remained very much on the fringes of the festivities that were inseparable from the founding of a college and had a very minor share of the treat at the first public commencement which was held on September 12, 1718. It was a splendid occasion which "quite floored the opposition." The reverend Mr. Davenport offered an excellent oration in Latin thanking God and Mr. Yale for their effective teamwork, and after Governor Saltonstall had delivered a second Latin oration the gentlemen were entertained at a sumptuous dinner in the college hall while the ladies were regaled in the library.

The university was fiercely orthodox. The men who

founded Yale had bolted from Massachusetts in a hot fit of spiritual pride, carrying their uncompromising views with them. Faculty members were not only required to swear an oath of loyalty to the Congregational Establishment but were under obligation to repeat the process at frequent intervals. This sternness was necessary to the defined purpose of the Collegiate School. It had been erected in defiance of liberal Harvard and for the raising of the clergy in adherence to an implacable piety, and all other considerations were scarcely relevant. No man's thoughts were his own. The Church Adamant owned every man's soul and judged it. The price of spiritual freedom was damnation — many chose it — until like Edward Dickinson of Amherst, to name only one, the contemplation of the ghastly possibilities of eternity, drove them to a late and reluctant conversion.

In New Haven parsons could order written confessions from individuals in the flock to be submitted to them and made public if they chose. The body of sturdy young men who were required to endure such excesses of discipline and demean themselves to such immodest and immoderate penances reacted as anyone might have expected. Yale students misbehaved. They drank and caroused and breached law and order. They fought with one another and set upon the townsfolk. People were injured and occasionally some were killed, while Jehovah presumably drowsed.

The curriculum was weighted heavily in favor of theology, ancient Hebrew and the classical languages, and the sciences were comprehended under the title of "Natural Philosophy" with some emphasis on logic. Students mouthed the ancient tongues from five in the morning until six in the evening and recited Rector Pierson's own system of natural philosophy, composed expressly for their benefit. Prayers were compulsory and incessant. As Professor Hearnshaw wrote of Oxford and Cambridge in the reign of George IV, Yale, like the ancestral institutions, "was capable of providing little education that was of any use to anyone except a prospective clergyman who wished to give his congregation the benefit of original translations from the Greek Testament."

Although by general agreement upperclassmen could not be subjected to corporal punishment, anyone and everyone could and did box a freshman's ears. The fagging system operated with brutal ferocity, freshmen being of course the victims. When little Oliver Wolcott the younger, later Secretary of the Treasury under George Washington, came up from Litchfield to matriculate at the age of thirteen he was quite undone at the sight of the shivering, gownless freshmen cowering under the orders and the staves of the sleek sophomores. They were so formidable that save that they wore no wigs they were scarcely to be distinguished from the tutors and the professors. Frightened and shocked, little Oliver turned his horse and rode back to Litchfield without ever dismounting, to wait until he was fourteen before venturing back to New Haven.

The professors ruled over the college but the tutors ruled over the students. They were the jackals of the senior faculty, tyrants and spies who listened at keyholes, suborned witnesses and made tale-bearing their purpose in life, keeping the students at bay by the constant threat of expulsion arising principally from suspicion cast upon their religious convictions. Proud as Lucifer, sprung from the dragon seed of theological discord, the army of undergraduates bore the yoke badly. The severity of the rule bred fire in the belly. It appears that with some exceptions, long hours spent in bone-chilling churches listening to hair-splitting sermons interspersed with sadistic metaphors merely gave Yale scholars a taste for hellfire and brimstone, to say nothing of noise. They swarmed to taverns and oyster houses and fought with the bargemen along the river, who loathed their arrogant, dandified ways. They armed themselves with a "bully club," an improvised mace, snatched from the hands of some town desperado, and displayed it as a symbol of their determination to dominate the city. They elected a "major bully" and invested him with a "banger," or gold-headed cane of office, and he was attended by his creature, the "minor bully," chosen for his puny physique in contrast to the majestic measurements of the major bully. "An hundred and fifty or one hundred and eighty young gentlemen students," sighed President Ezra Stiles, in the pages of his diary, "is a bundle of wildfire, not easily controlled and governed and at best the diadem of a president is a crown of thorns."

Besides the miseries inflicted upon them by the tutors the students had other causes for complaint during Yale's first uncomfortable century. In spite of the energetic efforts of Cotton Mather, Jeremiah Dummer and other well-wishers, the college was drearily poor while heterodox

Harvard to the north was growing richer every day. The college abutted on the unsavory neighborhood of an almshouse, several taverns and the public jail, which also did duty as the local bedlam and debtor's prison. The students were distracted from the pursuit of knowledge and truth by the oaths and outcries of felons and madmen, and these no doubt did not find their confinement eased by the continuous bawling of hymns and prayers audible from the college and from which there was no prospect of escape. Improvements were made but they were slight and slow to come. Money came in dribs and drabs, a lottery here, prize money from a French frigate there, while the students shivered in winter and yawned and fretted throughout the hot, green summer, for the most part ill fed, ill housed and ill clothed.

When there was nothing better to do — a frequent state of affairs — the students rioted. In between riots and prayers, with the devil at their elbows they founded debating clubs. William Wickham founded the Linonian Society in 1753 "for the promotion of Friendship, and social intercourse, and for the advancement of Literature." The Brothers in Unity sprang up "for the improvement of science and friendship." They discussed whether a finite nature could commit an infinite crime and the suitability of imposing a tax on old maids. "Is it right to enslave Africans?" they asked, and "Does the soul always think?" Debates led to riots and sometimes to theatricals. In 1772 two irrepressible members of Linonia, James Hillhouse and Nathan Hale, presented for public view *The Beaux' Stratagem*, dragging the morals of New Haven to the level of those of London. This impious diversion was attended by ladies whose pure minds were instantly corrupted as was proved by their eagerness to attend the performance. Driven to harsh measures by the degeneracy of the times, the faculty put an end to the dramatic presentations — or tried to — but the end was merely finite. After a short period of abstinence and boredom the debaters were back on the stage again.

Yale was shaped and strung in the eighteenth century by puritans, libertines, scholars, beggars, martyrs and fanatics. Out of its chilly, smoky halls, where poor students slept on benches and cooked meager meals between lectures, out of the scrounging and the money-grubbing and the psalm-singing, a college, against all the laws of probability, was growing. In less than two hundred years from its founding it would become a university. In the meantime, having struggled through the eighteenth century, it set its sails for the imperial waters of the nineteenth.

For the eighteenth century, as centuries must, came to an end. Centuries take an unconscionable time a-dying and the age of reason and enlightenment was still squirming in its cerements when the "bullies" rioted once more in 1841, although Queen Victoria had ascended the throne of England and the new era had long put off its mourning for the old. But Yale clung to its riots. The students had rebelled against mathematics and had inaugurated a rite called the Burial of Euclid which kept them happy, occupied and in noisy mischief on an annual basis every autumn. They held a famous riot called the Conic Sections Rebellion in 1825 and they rebelled against the food in the refectory in the Bread and Butter Rebellion of 1828.

These events all took place during the protracted administration of Jeremiah Day, the president whose task it was
to pilot the college through the uneasy period that followed
the war of the Rebellion. These were restless times, and
for Day, a steady, gentle, conservative man, the difficulties
must have been enormous. To begin with, as the century
turned the old Jehovah began to show signs of senility,
having like Ahriman, the diabolic facet of his creator
Ahura Mazda of the ancient Persians, "created a creation
by which he made his own body more evil that [in the
end] he might be powerless."

Day, although he accepted unequivocally the authority
of the church of his fathers and, as all presidents of Yale
were required to do, held orders in it, was a mathematician.
He wrote an algebra which saw service in American schools
for a century or more, and during his forty-five years in
office kept a weather log of New Haven, creating a pre-
cedent which all subsequent presidents of Yale have followed. He was a sweet-natured, contemplative man who
took his time about things. His courting of Roger Sherman's desirable daughter, Martha ("Patty"), was so un-
impetuous that Benjamin Silliman warned him in 1801 that
the stern Squire Sherman was growing restive and that this
gentle suitor must move with more speed if he did not
wish to lose the race. The warning produced results but
did not permanently alter Day's habits. Under Day's
deliberate rule, the longest in the history of Yale, college
prayers which had hitherto been prolonged, became inter-
minable. The suffering students, in forced attendance,
shuffled, coughed and whispered, tracked mud into the
chapel and lurked at the doors in order to be the first to

bolt when, if ever, the president should temporarily put an end to his colloquy with the Almighty.

Day's prayers they are delightful,
They last from morn to nightfall,
And when to pray Day's once begun
Day never stops till Day is done,

lamented the students in the eighteen-forties. Undeterred, President Day prayed on. He was dapper and old-fashioned and he patronized the same wigmaker for fifty years, embarrassing his children and grandchildren by wearing a red wig, slightly too large for him, to chapel, where it slipped rakishly over one eye during Divine Service.

Day had four children, a son by Martha Sherman and three daughters by his second wife, Olivia Jones. By the time these children were born the fierce climate of the founding fathers with its religious enthusiasm and its tavern brawling was yielding to the distracting influences of the Industrial Revolution and the romantic era. Calvinism was beginning to undergo a change and a softening and from being tragic and abrasive had become sentimental and melancholy. The students at Andover Theological Seminary moped and quarreled with their food while reading divinity and wallowed in bootless introspection, which must have been tedious and comfortless in about equal degrees.

"They [the students of Andover] are worn out with mere feeling," complained Leonard Bacon in 1822. "They are very conscientious but their notions of duty are incorrect. If they would but check feeling and substitute princip[le] and attend to the business immediately before them they would soon be relieved of their dyspepsia and hypochondria and accomplish about twice as much study and acquire about four times as much knowledge." "And now," he concluded, "see what a little resolution will do! I have written this letter in less time than I spent groaning about it." Bacon was not a man to take his own counsel easily, and being a child of his age he indulged in at least as much misery and hypochondria as anyone else.

"A dark day — a day of gloom and insufficiency . . . my health is poor and have reason to think it will never be better. I believe my activity is pretty near a close if not my mortal existence." The extent of his moodiness may be gauged from the fact that this passage was written with sixty years of unceasing activity ahead of him, including the begetting of fourteen children and the espousal of such causes as antislavery, the conversion of China, universal temperance and the defense of Henry Ward Beecher in his trial for adultery.

Young men indulged in fevers and raptures, young women dreamed of reforming Lord Byron. The romantic era was also the era of abolition and the Irish famine. In New Haven a Beethoven society flourished as well as a station of the underground railroad and a growing demand for more and better education for women. Woman dabbled in science and religion and wrote verses. The first Mrs. Lyman Beecher, with her immense family and her roaring boy of a husband clinging to her skirts, dropped cooking and mending and ignored the wails of the newest Beecher to share with a friend the exciting news "of the discovery that fixed alkalies are metallic oxyds."

The Beecher women interfered with chemistry and, what

was worse, they interfered with God, prying into the arc of the Lord and setting up in opposition to the best authorities on predestination, free will, infant damnation and other absorbing subjects. They agreed that if God destroyed the infants of Sodom he intended to make it up to them in another world and that God did not demand of men what they could not carry out or endure. In 1836 Catharine Beecher published her refutation of Jonathan Edwards on the Will. It was a frightening thing to do and scared a German professor of divinity very badly. "A woman! Refute Edwards on the Will! God forgive Christopher Columbus for discovering such a country."

Under the elm trees and horse chestnuts of New Haven and past the pretty doorways with their fanlights and the fragrant lilacs nodding on either side of the pillared porches, little ten-year-old girls frisked and frolicked on their way to Miss Tucker's school in 1837. Miss Prudence Crandall had opened a school "for young ladies and little misses of color" in Canterbury in 1833, but the less liberal element in the town had stoned the school and threatened to fire the premises and eventually disposed of the young ladies and little misses by putting their headmistress in jail. So the young ladies pursued their studies at Miss Tucker's. There was Rebecca Hatch Bacon, goddaughter and namesake to Mrs. Nathaniel Taylor, whose husband, the professor of didactic theology at the college had worsted Bennet Tyler in a famous controversy over the freedom of the will. There were Frances Chamberlin, "a great girl of twelve," and Julia Dwight, Sarah Tyler, Lizzie Baldwin, Lizzie Thacher, Henrietta Blake and Olivia Day. The young ladies of Miss Tucker's academy had before them several alarming examples of female attainment. Rebecca's burning-eyed aunt, Delia Bacon, was shortly to dispense large doses of classical and Renaissance history to the admiration of the gentility in a series of levees held in her rooms and was already the author of several romances and a drama in verse. Olivia Day's sister Martha, who had died aged twenty in 1833, had been an accomplished classical scholar and had believed that "Plato could be read with profit by any Christian."

Martha Day had been a sprightly, dark girl, looking younger than her actual years, living in a world that "was altogether different from that inhabited by common minds." Along with the classics she read Hebrew, French and German with ease and when she was fifteen had become a founder member of a New Haven literary society for ladies. She exhibited a breadth of literary understanding and a refinement of taste astonishing in so young a girl even in New England, where child prodigies were not uncommon. She wrote poetry, as she put it, when she "had not time for prose." She admired Byron and Wordsworth and loved Coleridge, from whom she thought she derived more benefit than from the study of Edwards on the Will. She dismissed Felicia Hemans in a sentence: "When the moral of a poem is evident a formal statement of it at the conclusion spoils the piece, at least to my mind." She dismissed herself with equal terseness. She would never write real poetry, she said. She made it clear in her letters and journals that she knew herself unequal to the heights of a Coleridge and did not aspire to those of Felicia Hemans. Religion, for which by her own admission she had neither taste nor talent, absorbed and obsessed her. She could not

shake the stifling embrace of the faith of her fathers even
while she deplored "the disgusting familiarity with which
Congregationalist ministers address God." She broke her
talent against her stony creed as though it had been glass,
declaring it to be valueless in the sight of God and therefore worthless in her own eyes.

> *Father, her heart from all her idols tearing,*
> *Thine erring child again would turn to thee,*
> *To thee she bends, trembling but not despairing*
> *From fear, remorse and sin, Oh Father, set her free.*

So saying, she horrified and edified New Haven by dying,
quickly and suddenly, of an unnamed ailment between
noon and midnight of a winter Sunday, her Sabbath task
of Bible teaching completed.

It was a classic death, a period piece, the kind of episode
that charged nineteenth-century literature with its charac-
teristic brand of sentiment. It is difficult to believe as we
read the ritualistic accounts of lives and deaths as they
occurred a hundred and fifty-odd years ago that these
events actually took place at all. The Player Queen protests too much, the actors saw the air and out-Herod
Herod. The effects are lifelike but not quite real. When
the mourners deliver themselves of their lines they can be
clearly heard in the last rows of posterity and the diction
is perfect.

"She is gone — gone — and there will never be another
such for us," lamented her friends. "She had been the
repository of my every thought and feeling. My greatest
happiness was not perfect without her sympathy."

"Weep not, she is not dead but sleepeth," intoned
Eleazar Fitch, one of the holy terrors of the Divinity

School, over her bier. Whatever Jeremiah Day may have felt he chose not to make it public. He was luckier than some parents. A son and two daughters remained to him, and Olivia, the elder of the two surviving girls, showed signs of a lively and even irreverent intelligence. Of all the girls attending Miss Tucker's school, Olivia was, with the exception of her dearest and sweetest friend, Henrietta Blake, the prettiest and most promising.

Miss Tucker's scholars formed an intricate branching of cousins and double cousins whose roots were solidly embedded in church, state and college. They bore family names stretching back principally to the wool staplers' guilds and the building trades of fourteenth-century England — Taylor and Sherman, Thacher and Tyler. They rejoiced in comfortable houses, affectionate parents, gay nurseries full of brothers and sisters, hams and turkeys and mince pies in the larder, cider in the cellar. They dressed in blue and scarlet merino with flounces of French lace. They dined richly at rich tables, wielding the family silver with grandparents who were signers of the Declaration of Independence, pastors and elders of the true church or senior professors at the college. Their names and birth dates were written in a spidery hand in family Bibles so heavy that a child could scarcely lift them. Education wearied them but they were good students.

"Miss Edwards says," wrote Henrietta Blake, "[that] practice makes perfect but I think that on every composition you write you bestow a small portion of brains and I think if you continue long in this bad practice that the brains are gradually worn out."

The girls complained of Miss Edwards, of long sermons

on Sundays, of Papa's wigs, especially the red one, of Latin and Greek, of people borrowing their paints and brushes without leave and failing to return them, of Blair's *Rhetoric*, Day's *Algebra* and Watts's *On the Mind*. "What a narrow escape I had from Watts' *On the Mind*," continued Henrietta, "that *fine, firm, invincible* book!"

The young people were wild for innocent fun. The harshness of earlier beliefs and practices was being sanded to smoothness in the war of attrition waged against them by the skepticism of a revolutionary age and by freedom of inquiry. Calvinist Yale, which had fought the production of stage plays, had in due course produced not only dramas but two Episcopal bishops as well. The doctrines of eternal punishment, the controversy over Salvation by Grace or the same by works, having undergone the agonized scrutiny of a previous generation, were now coming to be less questioned than ignored. Unmindful of the state of their souls, undergraduates organized skating parties, boating excursions and ultimately balls. There were strawberry fêtes with fireworks and cold salmon on the Fourth of July and merrymaking at Christmas as set forth in the pages of Mr. Dickens and only lately countenanced in Cromwellian Connecticut. Jonathan Edwards had once been known to have purchased a child's toy for one of his children. New Haven children in the eighteen-forties had not only toys and paintboxes but pets. "Oh my kitten," chirrupped Henrietta Blake, "thou eatest the dew of the morning and drinkest the fat of the land." Miss Tucker had a high regard for pearls of speech.

Miss Tucker offered on the whole a good education.

Her students left her school at the age of eighteen or there-
abouts, instructed in the classics, agile in the use of their
own language, and versed in the elements of mathematics,
logic and rhetoric. They had also read a little philosophy
and a little chemistry. Had they been men they would
have for the most part gone to Yale and become clergymen,
although a few might have chosen to become surgeons,
lawyers or scientists. A few of Miss Tucker's pupils,
Rebecca Hatch Bacon, for one, prevailed on Professor
Benjamin Silliman to lecture to them on chemistry. Another
group collected a lecturer in history to instruct them in a
parlor in Chapel Street. The young ladies organized *con-
versazioni*, musicales and taught Sunday School while waiting to marry. In most cases they would marry clergymen.
It was the common fate, and the majority of girls antici-
pated it with pleasure. In the meantime they could flirt
and dress and pray or otherwise improve themselves and
envy their brothers and their beaux their superior privileges.
They viewed the events and disorders of the college from
the outside, like pauper children flattening their noses
against the glass of a bakery window.

New England winters are long and cold, and for those
without a fixed occupation boring. February is the bleakest
and most disheartening month of the year, with Christmas
far behind and spring, like a long-distance runner, pacing
ahead and not to be overtaken. In the February of 1846
the college was undergoing a crisis over rules governing
the taking of books from the library. This engrossing concern, which was fraught with every kind of difficulty, was
hotly discussed by students and faculty alike and by the

debating clubs, Linonia and the Brothers in Unity. The third of these societies, Calliopean, composed mainly of Southerners, never degenerated to this subject — indeed, never appears to have degenerated to any subject whatever, but merely uttered aristocratic noises in favor of honor and horseflesh. Dean Theodore Dwight Woolsey was in Greece. There was a minor riot and the faculty announced its intention of forming a college police force. Professor Josiah Willard Gibbs of the theological department was promoted to the office of graduated reader in the Brothers society and a new emblem was prepared for Skull and Bones to replace a damaged one. Some unquenchable sophomores put on a skit which was not only profane but also made fun of President Day. The tutors continued to be much what they had always been, spies and tale-bearers. The students showed no improvement either but remained noisy, slovenly, bored, attending to anything rather than their prayers and their studies, although one serious student had prepared for publication in the *Yale Literary Magazine* an article entitled "The Progress of Civilization." And as if there were not enough printed matter emanating from Yale, a new publication, palpably springing from a source within the college, made an appearance. The thing was a newspaper, set up with headlines and a high editorial purpose. It was printed by D. C. Gilman and ran to several pages of newsprint. It bore a rather tantalizing name — *The Gallinipper* — and nobody seemed to know what this piece of gibberish stood for. The motto *Magna est Gallinipper et prevalebit* which served to introduce the first editorial did not clarify matters. Nor did the statement of aims and ideals throw any light on the identity of either editors or contributors, although the manner of writing and the knowledgeability concerning college affairs exhibited by the unknown journalists showed that the publication was the work of persons intimate with Yale. Almost certainly one more undergraduate prank was afoot. The first shot was a piece of unparalleled impertinence.

> *We would not inflict upon our readers an apology for our undertaking* [declared the editors], *nor would we try them with a tedious statement of reasons for introducing a new publication into our college world. Suffice it to say that having observed the prevailing taste for a style of literature, different from that at present among us and feeling the necessity for a college* journal *we resolved upon using our efforts to supply the deficiency ... Our Plan is a simple one. We shall merely report the sayings and doings in and about the college. A portion of the papers shall be devoted to reports from the different literary societies with accounts of the debates and the persons who figure therein.*
>
> *In short we intend assuming a general supervision over the college.*

The final paragraph hinted at but gave no clue to the identity of the writers.

> *In parting with this our first number, we advise you, oh readers, to refrain from troubling your wits to find out who or what we are: for you will never discover more than this.*
>
> *We three brothers be*
> *In one mysterious unity.*

Having thus whetted the curiosity of its readers *The Gallinipper* spat on its hands and proceeded to a lively account of the debate in Linonia "On the Expediency of Entering the Library Building." A Mr. Case began with an objection, he "thought after we once were in we should never be able to get out." A Mr. Steele "thought it would be just as easy to move the books out after they were once in as it was now to move them in. . . . (Horses and carts would be available and the society would pay.) He had introduced this resolution because he thought it necessary to leave some record to show that the library had been moved by the proper authorities and not by stealth." Mr. Coon, a junior, "thought that the best way would be to take the faculty in a body before the Governor and make them swear to keep their hands from picking and stealing."

The Gallinipper's agents were everywhere and they reported the Brothers in Unity on the same subject, punning remorselessly on the names of the members. The Calliopean Society was presented in the throes of permanent self-adoration and appeared to have discussed nothing save itself: "The noonday sun sheds not more resplendent rays on the broad earth than does Calliope on our college world. The pale moon from the time she first appears glimmering in the far west, waxes not more rapidly to the full than has Calliope to station and eminence."

The issue contained further an unfavorable criticism on a sophomore skit on the grounds that it mingled the sacred with the profane and ridiculed President Day in a heartless manner. There was an announcement of a new chair of

history and a list of the lectures that it should body forth:
these included "A filial contemplation of Adam in his
paternal relation to mankind. Influence of the climate and
situation of Eden upon his character. Topographical survey
of the land of Nod." The series dragged in "Moses, the
man of his age," and concluded with "A philosophic view
of Socrates in his domestic relations." Contributors were
advised to direct their material to O.Z. at Yale College
and the whole issue was embellished with little drawings,
of which the most significant was a view of an insect seated
in an armchair with its feet on a desk.

The February issue was scarcely off the press when it
was succeeded by the March number and the paper's early
promise was more than realized. A contributor writing
under the name of Thomas Carlyle produced the first of
what purported to be a series of "Sketches of the Faculty"
and undertook the biography of a tutor Azariah Eldridge,
or "Eldrudge," as the writer insisted on spelling his victim's
name.

> *His name Azariah, with the eyes of him a grey-*
> *color, or rather a no-color and a mouth by no means*
> *inexpressive; the reader is particularly desired to note*
> *this man; this is the tutor Eldrudge, a man worth*
> *looking at. . . .*
> *Azariah learned to write, and a specimen of his*
> *Epistolary success might be adduced; it is addressed*
> *to his Pylades, Pythias, Jonathan, Pollux or whoever*
> *it may be and is this, —*
> *Dear Frend,*
> *I am well and hope you are the same. We have*

first rate fun at speling school and sinin school this winter. Betsey spelt me down. Do you know Wells?
                                        Your frend
                                                    A. E.

This twelve-year-old letter is a Stepping Stone across Abysmal Obscurities and Transition Stages and Chaotic Conditions to his emergement into light at a certain Do-the-boys Hall where . . . find Azariah a tutor, not a Wackford Squeers at a larger Do-the-Boys. But no treacles and Smikisms for him; the soul of him is a human soul; his great heart beats for the smallest form of freshman humanity.

The tutor having been disposed of, the editors turned to correspondence and news. Professor Woolsey was in Greece where "many inquiries were made about *The Gallinipper* and much curiosity expressed to see it. . . . The Prof. sent a copy to his hostess and each of her guests and writes that the former who is perfectly acquainted with English is so delighted with it that she has translated it into Greek for the amusement of her countrymen."

Dean Woolsey was not the only member of the faculty who expressed himself as delighted with *The Gallinipper*. The correspondence column contained the following:

Dear Gall. —
I wish you would have the goodness to convey the following instructions to the students of Yale through the medium of your valuable periodical. But first allow me to say something relative to your paper itself. I regard it as a most desirable publication — one that I have felt the need of in our institution ever since I

*had the honor of being its head, and I hope you will
by all means keep it up. If you please put me down
as a subscriber for six copies and permit me to say that
I shall use my influence to have every member of the
faculty take it also. There is one caution which I hope
you will observe; in the Sketches of the Faculty which
you propose giving, you had better be careful and not
bring to light too many of our sprees, as it might have
a demoralizing influence on the college. (This is an
idea which had occurred to us and which we shall
certainly act upon — Eds. Gall.) Hurrah for the
Gallinipper!*

Affectionately yours —
<small>Jeremiah —</small>

*P.S. What do you say to a little oyster supper some
night at Tucker's where we can drink success to your
paper. I'm there if you say so and will treat with the
greatest pleasure, only nothing stronger than ale,
mind you. I never spree nowadays.*

This gratifying communication was followed by President Day's "Hints to the students of Yale for the regulation of their deportment during college prayers":

*"Never think of starting until the second bell turns
over. If in the morning do not stop to dress: it is
generally expedient to put on a cloak and boots but
no more is requisite; above all do not wash or comb
your hair, or you might be thought foppish . . . rush
up the aisles in a crowd and find your seats with the
greatest possible noise . . . when in your seat assume a
horizontal position . . . go to sleep . . . whisper with
your neighbors. If on a Sunday evening study the
galleries to see what ladies are there. In short do anything rather than listen to the reading. That is de-*

*signed to divert the faculty and give you a chance to
enjoy yourselves. [At] the time of the prayers . . .
your duty commences in earnest . . . crack jokes with
your right and left hand neighbors . . . notify everyone of your presence who is within reach of your
hands and feet . . . keep up a brisk circulation of pea-
nuts. It is a very good plan to bring in a bat which
can be let loose if things seem to be getting dull or if
that cannot be obtained a dog will answer the purpose
just as well. Whistle him from one seat to another and
by pinching his ears, treading on his toes, and various
other means which will suggest themselves with the
occasion, extract as much noise from him as he . . . is
capable of. Dogs were principally made for this purpose. . . . If these regulations are observed they cannot
fail to make you patterns of dignified and gentle-
manly conduct and if adhered to through life, will
ensure you the respect of all society.*

With the president's invitation in its pocket and prayers
out of the way the editors of *The Gallinipper* proceeded
to the scrutiny of the *Yale Literary*, a rival publication, for
which it professed an admiration bordering on reverence.

*We have just risen from an earnest perusal of the
last number of this — the pride and boast of our
college — and really words are faint and so are we —
in fact we fainted several times before we finished
our task. We have formerly spoken several times of
the high character which the Yale Literary sustains
both at home and abroad. Yet this time it has outdone
itself — so learned — so philosophical — so original —
but we must let it speak its own praises.*

The contribution entitled The Progress of Civilization *has struck us as one of uncommon merit. It may*

be taken as a superior specimen of the usual articles which fill this high-toned magazine and as such we shall make it its principal representative, and proceed to illustrate —

The Learning of the Yale Literary —

. . . "A very ancient nation built the pyramids" . . . how much research and midnight oil must have been expended at arriving at these facts! . . . Listen, O ye Freshmen! "Romulus was a Greek." . . . We lay our hand on our mouth and pass. We are told as another fact that "The Roman Nation fell" and lastly that "missionaries are now quite numerous." We the editors of the Gallinipper fainted unanimously when we came to this last announcement, we did indeed.

Recovering from their swoon the three mysterious brothers proceeded to the attack on "The Philosophy of the Yale Literary" also embodied in "The Progress of Civilization."

The Egyptians . . . developed the idea of reverence, the Greeks of beauty, the Romans of he does not know exactly what, about which time the Christian Religion rushing in produced the Dark Ages. . . . Not being exactly clear as to the way in which progress was promoted in the Dark Ages he leaps across them and lands in the middle of the nineteenth century, where looking around he declares that as there is a spirit of enterprize abroad and things are better now than they used to be there must have been progress and he believes that there has been.

If learning and philosophy suffered at the hands of the editors of *The Gallinippers*, their fate was mild by comparison with that which befell Poetry. A rash undergraduate gave to the world a minor epic called "The Origin of the Robin Red-Breast," pretending to be an adaptation of an Indian legend. It concerned an Indian brave:

> *In mystic lore he should excel*
> *And prophesy extremely well.*

For some obscure reason the brave after a number of seemingly disconnected adventures is turned into a robin, thus proving with no visible reason the efficacy of filial obedience. At the hands of *The Gallinippers* the redskin bit the dust. "We feel sure that all who read this attractive presentation of the duty will practice this obedience although they may not be so fortunate as to turn into robin red-breasts."

They concluded their demolition of the *Literary* by taking sentences and subjecting them to an analysis worthy of the grammar class at Miss Tucker's school.

> *"By seeking too soon to mature the mind we suppress the rich play of fancy, wither the early blossoms of affection and hurry the intellect itself to death like a breathless stag."*
> *Prove that a breathless stag, by seeking too soon to mature his mind does restrain himself in this unnatural and dangerous manner. (Eds.)*

> *"Pure genuine culture disappears under the mechanical process of learning by rote mere forms of grammatical niceties."*
> *Prove that grammatical niceties have curbed the genius of the Yale Literary.*

And having made good on their promise to produce a genuine college journal *The Gallinipper* subsided for nearly two years.

It had aroused considerable speculation, and some anger. The biography of Tutor Eldridge had bordered on the disrespectful. The bandying about of the names of President Day and Dean Woolsey was not considered funny. Quips at the expense of the senior societies and lampoons on the Doxology such as the one that concluded a ballad on "The Burial of Euclid" were construed to be nearly as damaging to student morals as the rite itself.

> *Praise Ives* you students, hard of Yale,*
> *Praise Ives from whom flows all our ale —*
> *Praise loud the facultatis lex —*
> *Praise spying tutors, Profs and Prex.*

In a phrase typical of the editors of *The Gallinipper* "a shudder walked through the room and out at the door which it closed deliberately behind it." But who had done this thing?

Suspicion fell upon Leonard Woolsey Bacon, whose father Leonard Bacon was about to engage in a deadly struggle with the faculty of the Divinity School over the alleged indecorum of his sister Delia in her relations with Nathaniel Taylor's protégé, Alexander MacWhorter. New Haven shook with the scandal. Eleazar Fitch's daughter, Jane, was bearing tales from doorstep to doorstep about Miss Bacon and was a principal witness in the inquiry concerning the scandal which was instituted between the Divinity School and the New Haven West Association

* Mr. Ives kept a tavern.

(the parish clergy). Implicated in the scandal, Henrietta Blake had taken herself to the country like a Roman princess, fallen into disfavor. She went with her cousin, Sarah Thacher, to the house of Deacon Calhoun. She found him "a perfect *gem*, [wearing] a black coat so short-waisted that the buttons come up on his shoulder-blades." She added in another letter to the same people, her sister, Mary and Mary's fiancé, that "I've retained the severe letter of Dr. Bacon that scared me into a meek preparation of heart for Miss Bacon's visit. I shall show it around on my return and let people judge for themselves."

Sarah wrote "I do feel for Jane Fitch. Do give my most sympathising love to Jane Fitch and tell her to *make an effort.*"

With the clergy at loggerheads and all the girls of New Haven, heads tossing and petticoats rustling, gabbling about it, with MacWhorter pouring out his woes to the governor of Connecticut, with Jane Fitch taking Sarah's advice and sparing no effort, the faculty of Yale College agreed to put an end to *The Gallinipper*. The Bacons were notorious pudding-sticks and Day and Woolsey decided at once where to find the source of the mischief. They called up young Leonard Woolsey Bacon and, without precisely accusing him of being author and publisher of the offending sheet, they informed him that if another issue appeared he and whoever might be described as his associates would be immediately rusticated. No further issues appeared in 1846 and nothing was forthcoming in 1847.

The Bacon-MacWhorter scandal died down. President Day retired and Dean Woolsey was named President of

Yale. In November of 1848 *The Gallinipper* struck again. It struck with a vengeance and at one person, a tutor named Lewis Raymond Hurlburt.

He was celebrated not only in the prose of "Thomas Carlyle" in a biographical sketch entitled "Hell-bird" as "a now six-hundred-a-year no-mindedness (great hoax from little acorns grow)" but in the coarse cruel verse of the editors of *The Gallinipper* themselves.

> *A young she-ass strolled forth one day,*
> *A merry scampering brute.*
> *The devil chanced to cross her way,*
> *Love-struck he lured the maid astray*
> *and Hurlburt was the fruit.*

The Gallinipper had two axes to grind, the espionage system under which the students groaned at the hands of the tutors and the secret societies which produced evils all of their own.

> *The most useless and virulent of all College ani-*
> *mosities is that arising from the Secret Societies. . . .*
> *A peculiar pin makes or mars the man and blinded by*
> *envy and venom the student sees nothing good or*
> *honest without the pale of his own society. Any*
> *member of an opposing society is branded as a knave*
> *or a fool, though he be high-minded or talented. . . .*
> *On being introduced into a society a man lays aside*
> *not only candor but truth and he who is otherwise a*
> *gentleman must fiercely lie or foully slander — lie*
> *that he may gloss over the knavery of his association,*
> *slander that he may throw odium on another and may*
> *be a better. . . . Would that these associations . . . could*
> *be swept away from Old Yale. Then and not till*

then the sons of a common Alma Mater will be
brothers indeed as well as in name.

As for the tutors, they suffered attacks that were both tedious and long-winded. There were parodies of Shakespeare, parodies of Byron and parodies of Scott in which the hated creatures were lampooned with witchlike persistence. And in case ridicule should miss the target the editors resorted to pure polemic and finally to a tone of sweet reasonableness addressed to the faculty.

They quoted a conversation overheard on the campus between a tutor and a member of the freshman class as an example of the lengths to which the spies would go to garner information.

> *"Do you know whether such-and-such persons are in the habit of using profane language?"*
> *"I do not."*
> *"Will you endeavor to find out and then tell me?"*
> *"I will."*
> *The consequences were that the individuals referred to were denied matriculation. . . . Our respected masters sometimes exercise power in a manner which we cannot approve. We give the faculty much credit for vigilance and we modestly claim the same compliment in return. Our knowledge of their secret councils is perhaps more extensive than they imagine.*

The last statement was indisputable. At least one of the editors of *The Gallinipper* was in a position to know nearly all that there was to be known about the administration of Yale College and two of the others moved freely enough within the circle of the very elect to be privy to most of its secrets.

Had the faculty taken more of an interest in either etymology or entomology they would have found a clue to the identity of the editors of the troublesome little newspaper in both these disciplines. The gallinipper is the female mosquito and it is she who delivers the sting. While Jeremiah Day, Theodore Dwight Woolsey, Josiah Willard Gibbs and Benjamin Silliman laid about them among the undergraduates for culprits to castigate *The Gallinipper* went to press from President Day's own parlor, edited by President Day's accomplished daughter Olivia, with the assistance of Henrietta Whitney Blake and the charming and lively Louisa Torrey. The faculty were correct in casting a baleful eye on Leonard Woolsey Bacon, who spared the young ladies the exertion of taking the paper to the printers by taking it to them himself. He was probably assisted by Charles T. H. Palmer and John Ball Brisbin, who were among the few writers in the *Yale Literary Magazine* who escaped a flaying at the hands of their sister journalists.

There is very little evidence that even as late as 1849 the real names of the "three brothers" were generally known. *The Gallinipper* was receiving more contributions than it could handle, however, and was kindly offering to send rejected material across the way to the *Literary*, which could no doubt make use of it. The next few issues, which appeared sporadically between 1849 and 1858, dealt with ever-increasing virulence with the problem of the tutor but ceased to attack the senior societies. The original editors resigned their posts, Olivia Day and Henrietta Blake to marry clergymen, Louisa Torrey to become the wife of

Alphonso Taft and subsequently the mother of President William Howard Taft.

The Gallinipper had struck at a very real evil under the editorship of the three girls. When they left the paper in the hands of undergraduates they provided the class of 1858 with a well-honed weapon against the evils of the "tutoric system" which survived like a living fossil from the days of the church's tyranny over the scholastic body. The tone of *The Gallinipper's* last issue in 1858 is vitriolic but also cocksure. The chief editorial likens the task of characterizing the tutor to that of dissecting a putrid corpse:

> *Look at him — his lank form hung about with rusty black, his gaunt and sallow face — his independent shock of hair which sometimes clings lovingly to his Praise-God-Barebones face. He is an abolitionist who favors amalgamation. He is the mons [monster] who brought forth the ridiculous mouse of our present marking system and the mover in faculty meetings of all those petty tyrannies of our college government. He prays to God that the standard of scholarship might be raised and lowers it himself by pretending to instruct. . . . If a student offend him he can cut him off from the college. . . . We should not have tutors placed over us . . . too young to know how to govern us well. . . . We wish to recite to none but professors.*

Whether or not *The Gallinipper* helped to abolish Praise-God-Barebones is questionable, but there is no doubt that it raised an independent voice and gave moral support and confidence to the student body at a time when it needed it badly. The change for the better was inevitable. The tutors went. Under the hand of Theodore Dwight

Woolsey, Yale moved inexorably toward its goal of becoming a university and the establishment of what the students of 1858 had pleaded for in the pages of *The Gallinipper*, "the English system."

The girls never gave up their secret but left it to their families to tell the story of their editorial triumphs. Olivia Day did not long survive hers. She married Thomas King Beecher in 1851, lived merrily with him for two years and died in childbirth in 1853. She had remained lighthearted and irreverent although immersed in a flood of Beechers and sent mocking letters to her cousin Julia Jones, advising her to abjure the horrors of the New England piety. Julia outlived Olivia to become the second Mrs. Thomas King Beecher and remained remorselessly religious until her death at the turn of the century.

Henrietta Blake made an honest man of the protagonist of the Bacon-MacWhorter scandal by marrying him and seeing to it that her father housed him for the duration of his life. Louisa Torrey mothered a President: Leonard Woolsey Bacon, whose efforts at least entitled him to honorable mention along with the names of the staff, became in due course a clergyman of unusual vehemence and originality. In the latter part of the nineteenth century he attempted singlehandedly to unify the Congregational church with the Anglican Communion and tried to prevail on the Archbishop of Canterbury to ordain him as a clergyman in the Church of England. His Grace refused on the grounds that although he himself was not averse to the idea he felt it would be anathema to his suffragans.

The Gallinipper, packed away in attics and basements,

lived on as a legend, a family joke in the Day "connexion." It found its way into letters exchanged between New Haven and Berkeley when Olivia's brother and niece moved west. Grand-aunts told young nieces of gay times in New Haven when Grandmama was young and even the President and the Dean couldn't guess who put out *The Gallinipper*.

The publication now lies preserved in the Yale Memorabilia collection along with its old enemy the *Literary*, which has long outlived it. *The Gallinipper* was impertinent, outrageous and occasionally vulgar. But there is vitality and anger in it. It is never querulous. Behind its parodies and polemics the smothered shriek of a healthy schoolgirl laughing at her betters whips through its tattered pages like the breeze off the sound through the elms of New Haven Green.

SELECTED READING LIST

SELECTED READING LIST

YOUR VENT'ROUS AFRIC

Various editions of the poems of Phillis Wheatley; *Letters of Phillis Wheatley* [including correspondence with Obour Tanner] (Boston: J. Wilson and Son, 1864); *Phillis Wheatley, Poems and Letters*, edited by Charles F. Heartman (New York: Privately printed, 1915); *Memoir of Phillis Wheatley, a Native African and a Slave* by B. B. Thatcher (Boston: George W. Light, 1834); *Memoir and Poems of Phillis Wheatley* by Margaretta Matilda Odell (Boston: George W. Light, 1834), in the Houghton Library, Harvard University; *The Countess of Huntingdon and Her Circle* by Sarah Tytler (London: Pitman, 1907); *An Essay on the Slavery and Commerce of the Human Species, Particularly the African* by Thomas Clarkson (London and Philadelphia: J. Cruikshank, 1786); *Methodism* by Rupert E. Davies (Harmondsworth, England: Penguin, 1963); *The Crusade against Slavery, 1830–1860* by Louis Filler (New York: Harper, 1960); *Black Cargoes* by Daniel Mannix in collaboration with Malcolm Cowley (New York: Viking, 1962); the published letters of Horace Walpole, Sancho's *Letters* (London: Printed for William Sancho, 1802); *The Interesting Narrative of the Life of*

Olaudah Equiano or Gustavus Vassa the African by Himself
(London: Printed for the Author, 1793); unpublished letters
and diaries of Martha Day; *The Cultural Life of the American
Colonies, 1607–1763* by Louis B. Wright (New York: Harper
Torchbooks, 1962).

THE WEEPING WILLOW AND THE ANTIMACASSAR

The published poems of Mary Howitt, Hannah Flagg Gould,
Felicia Dorothea Hemans, Joseph Rodman Drake, Fitz-Grene
Halleck; published letters of Jane Welsh Carlyle, Edgar Allan
Poe, Mrs. Hannah More; unpublished correspondence of the
Beecher family; essays by Lydia Maria Child; random selec-
tions from the published works of Lydia Huntley Sigourney;
The Poetical Works of Mrs. Felicia Hemans edited with a
critical memoir by William Michael Rossetti (London: E.
Moxon, Son & Co., 1873); *The Sweet Singer of Hartford* by
Gordon Haight (New Haven: Yale, 1930); *The Fathers of the
Victorians* by Ford K. Brown (Cambridge, Eng.: Cambridge,
1961); *The Cultural Life of the New Nation* by Russel Blaine
Nye (New York: Harper Torchbooks).

THE PARSON AND THE BLUESTOCKING

Delia Bacon by Theodore Bacon (Boston and New York:
Houghton, Mifflin, 1888); *The Philosophy of the Plays of
Shakespere Unfolded* by Delia Bacon (London: Grombridge
and Sons, 1857): *The Square Pegs* by Irving Wallace (New
York: Knopf, 1957); various sermons by Alexander Mac-
Whorter in the Sterling Memorial Library, Yale University;
"Recollections of a Gifted Woman," in *Our Old Home and
English Notebooks* by Nathaniel Hawtorne (Boston: Hough-
ton Mifflin, 1887); *Recollections of Seventy Years* by Eliza
Farrar (Boston: Ticknor and Fields, 1886); *Saints, Sinners and*

Beechers by Lyman Beecher Stowe (Indianapolis: Bobbs-Merrill, 1934); unpublished papers of the Beecher family and of the Blake family; the published sermons and correspondence of Leonard Bacon; unpublished correspondence of Leonard Bacon and Elizabeth Peabody; *The New Haven Register* for 1846–1847.

MISS BEECHER IN HELL

The Puritan Mind by Herbert W. Schneider (New York: Holt, 1930); *Jonathan Edwards* by Perry Miller (New York: Sloane, 1949); *The New England Mind: From Colony to Province* (Cambridge: Harvard, 1953) and *From the Seventeenth Century* (Cambridge: Harvard, 1954) by Perry Miller: *Sermons* by Jonathan Edwards (Hartford, Conn.: Hudson and Goodwin, 1780), "The Rational Account of the Main Doctrines of the Christian Religion Attempted" is in this collection; *Images or Shadows of Divine Things* edited by Perry Miller (New Haven: Yale, 1948); *The Minister's Wooing* by Harriet Beecher Stowe (Boston and New York (Houghton, Mifflin, 1896), Riverside Edition; and the unpublished papers of Alexander Metcalf Fisher.

GOD AND WOMAN AT YALE

The Gallinipper for February 1846–January 1858, in the Yale Memorabilia collection, Yale University; *The Memorial Quadrangle: A Book about Yale* compiled by Robert Dudley French (New Haven: Yale, 1929): *A Sketch of the History of Yale College* by James Luce Kingsley (Boston: Perkins, Marvin, and Co., 1835); *The New Haven Genealogical Magazine: Families of Ancient New Haven* by Donald J. Jacobus, 8 vols. (New Haven: Jacobus, 1922–32); *A Statistical Account of the City* of *New Haven* by Timothy Dwight (1811; reprint from the *New Haven City Year Book* for 1874, published in New Haven [?], 1875); in the Boston Athenaeum; minutes of the Old Colony Historical Society, Taunton, Massachusetts; *Annals of Yale College to 1831* by Ebenezer Baldwin (New Haven: Henry Howe, 1831); *The Blakes of 77 Elm Street* by Alida Blake Hazard (New Haven: Quinnipiak Press, 1924); and the unpublished correspondence of the Day family.